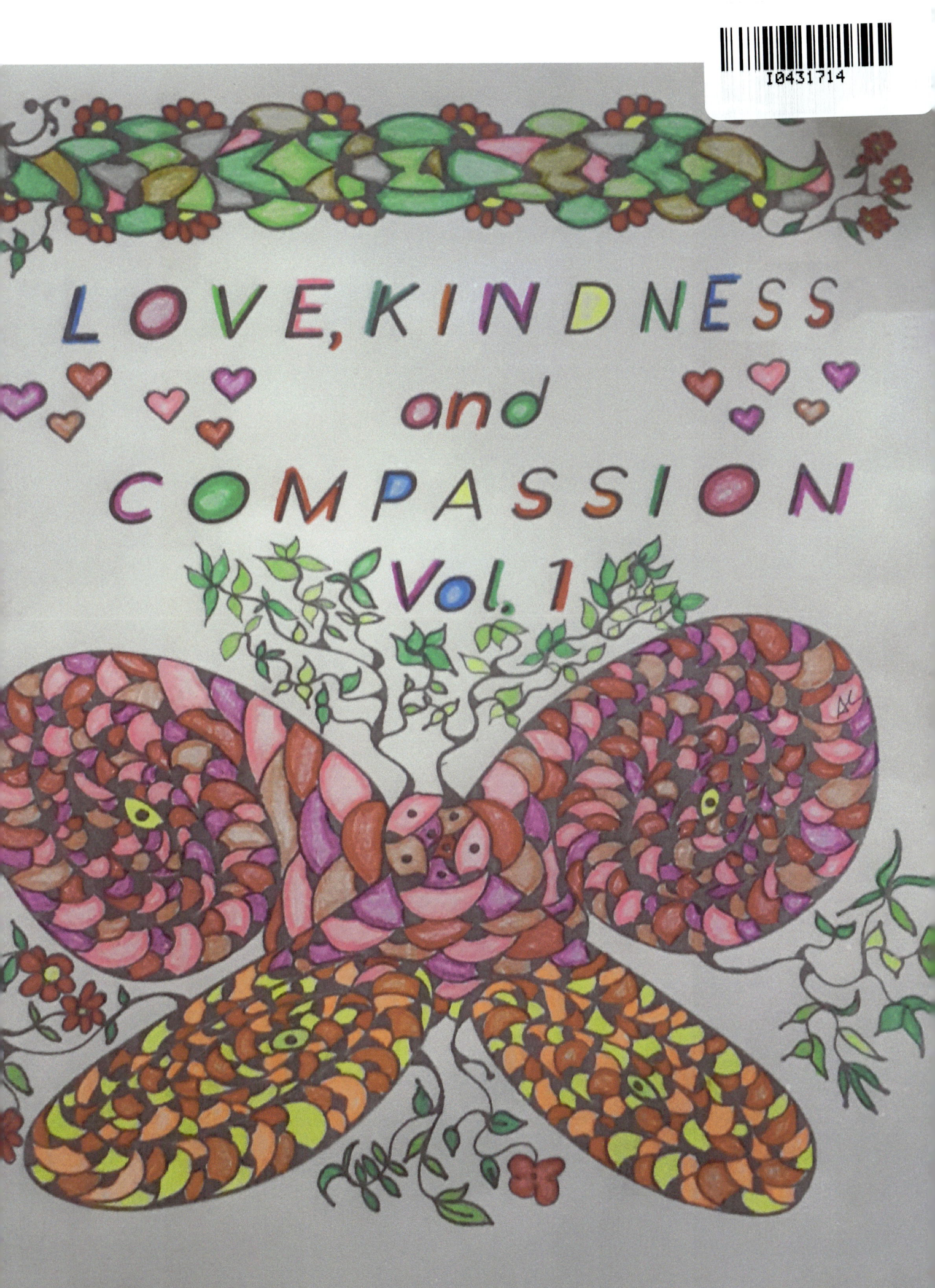

Learned to Love Myself presents:

    A Mental Health Break. Artwork by Annette Chiappe
    Love, Kindness and Compassion Vol. 1, *"Love"*

Copyright © 2019 by Annette Chiappe
First paperback printing, May 2019

All rights reserved. This book may not be reproduced in whole or in part, stored in a retrieval system, or transmitted in any form or by any means electronic, mechanical, or other without written permission from the author.

Cover design, Interior designs and Quotes by Annette Chiappe

ISBN: 978-1-9991111-0-6
Originally self- published in Canada

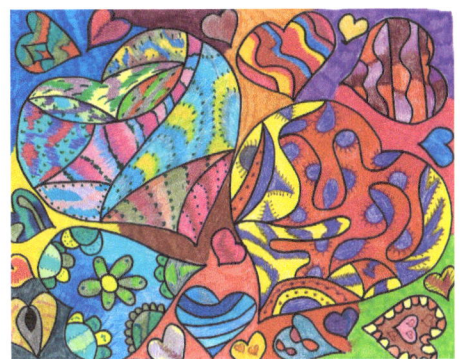

LOVE, KINDNESS AND COMPASSION, VOL. 1

Welcome to my first Colouring Book: Love, Kindness and Compassion Vol 1. *"Love"*

I am a Human Whisperer* and Warrior who dances to her own tune. I discovered, as a child, the true joy of timeless hours of drawing and colouring. I would disappear into the pages.

This book was created from healing my mental health issues. My spiritual teachers of Love, Kindness and Compassion John Lennon, Barbra Streisand, Oprah Winfrey, Prem Rawat, Eckhart Tolle, Deepak Chopra and the Dalai Lama inspired me to *Know Thy Self*. From their wisest messages, they guided my healing and influenced me to take up my pens and create from my soul.

It took me years of unlearning who I thought I was and then to accept love into my life. As a nanny, children taught me to be emergent* with life, to give myself permission to create and make things my own, like passion, courage and God. I eventually came out of my cocoon and tried out my new wings.

I believe that within each of us is an unbelievable creator and that colouring, puzzles, painting and all forms of Art are our personal healers. The reason I create is to inspire and fill the world with Love, Kindness and Compassion. These drawings represent my Spirit. I hope they give your inner child and adult self joy making these pages yours to love. Please share them with others as a small gift of gratitude and love.

DEDICATION

I am deeply blessed and grateful to Jan Hanley, my spiritual "sister from another mister", as we have coined it, for all the awareness she has taught me this book became possible. She taught and helped me to never give up on myself and to break through the barriers of post-traumatic stress *"disorder"*.
I would also like to thank all the loving souls who inspired and motivated me to be all that I am today. For love, kindness and compassion I thank Dave Turberfield, Daniel McDougall, Faith Schaffer, Jill Holliday, Tamara Thompson, Crystal Cumming and my loving and supportive life partner, Walter T. Moore.

Emergent - in the process of coming into or becoming prominent.

Human Whisperer - a person who uses a technique in which they "hold the space". That means that they listen to someone by being totally present; it means giving their heart, love and full attention to the other person

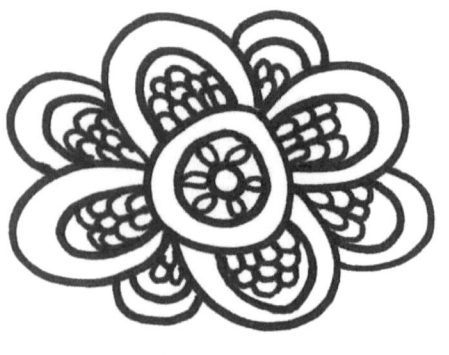
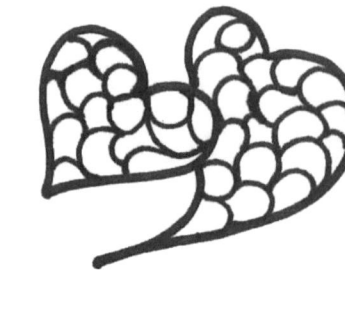

Can relaxing over a cup of warm coffee be Love?

What about dancing? Or, laughter with family?

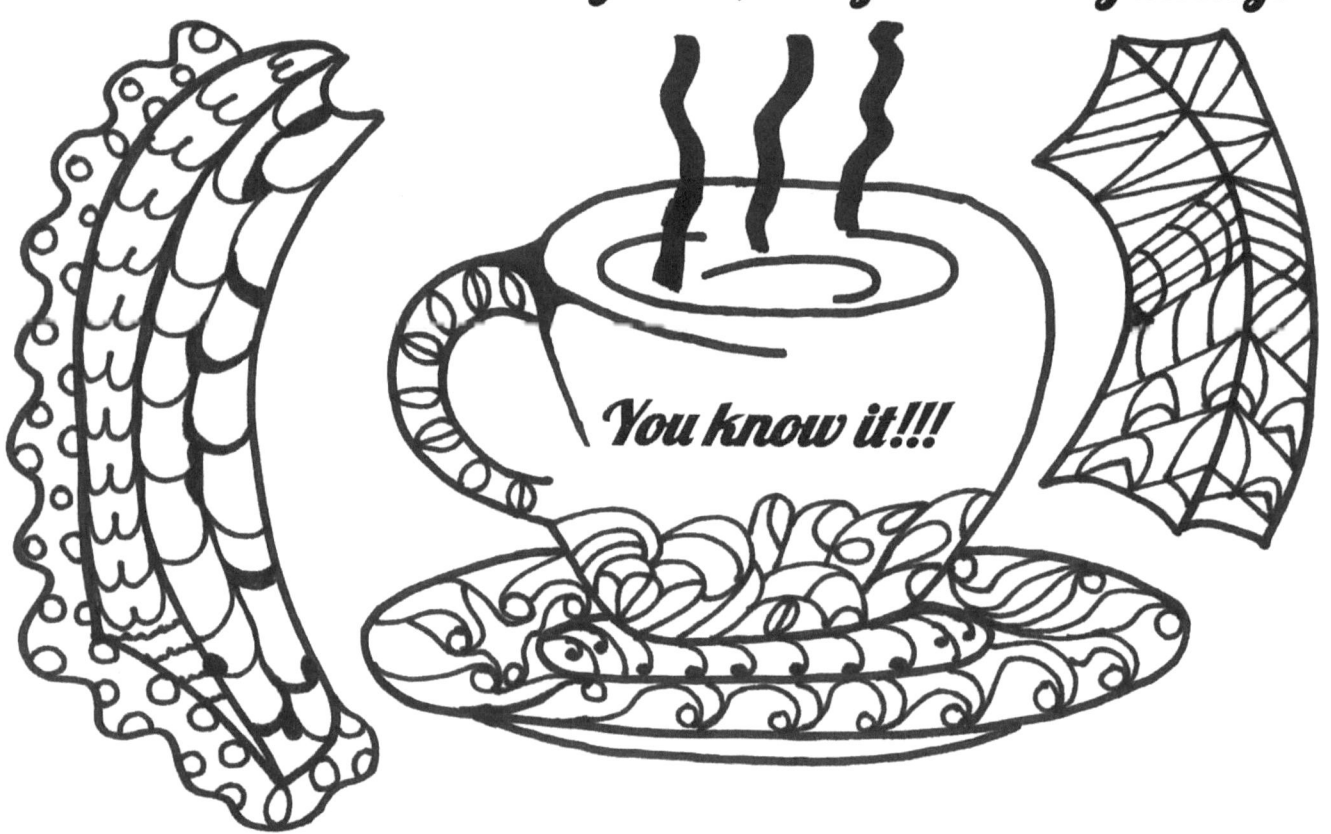

You know it!!!

So many little things bring joy into our hearts.

Make time for some today!

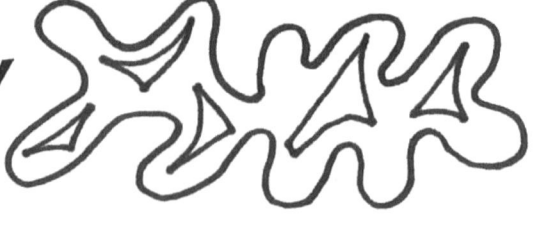

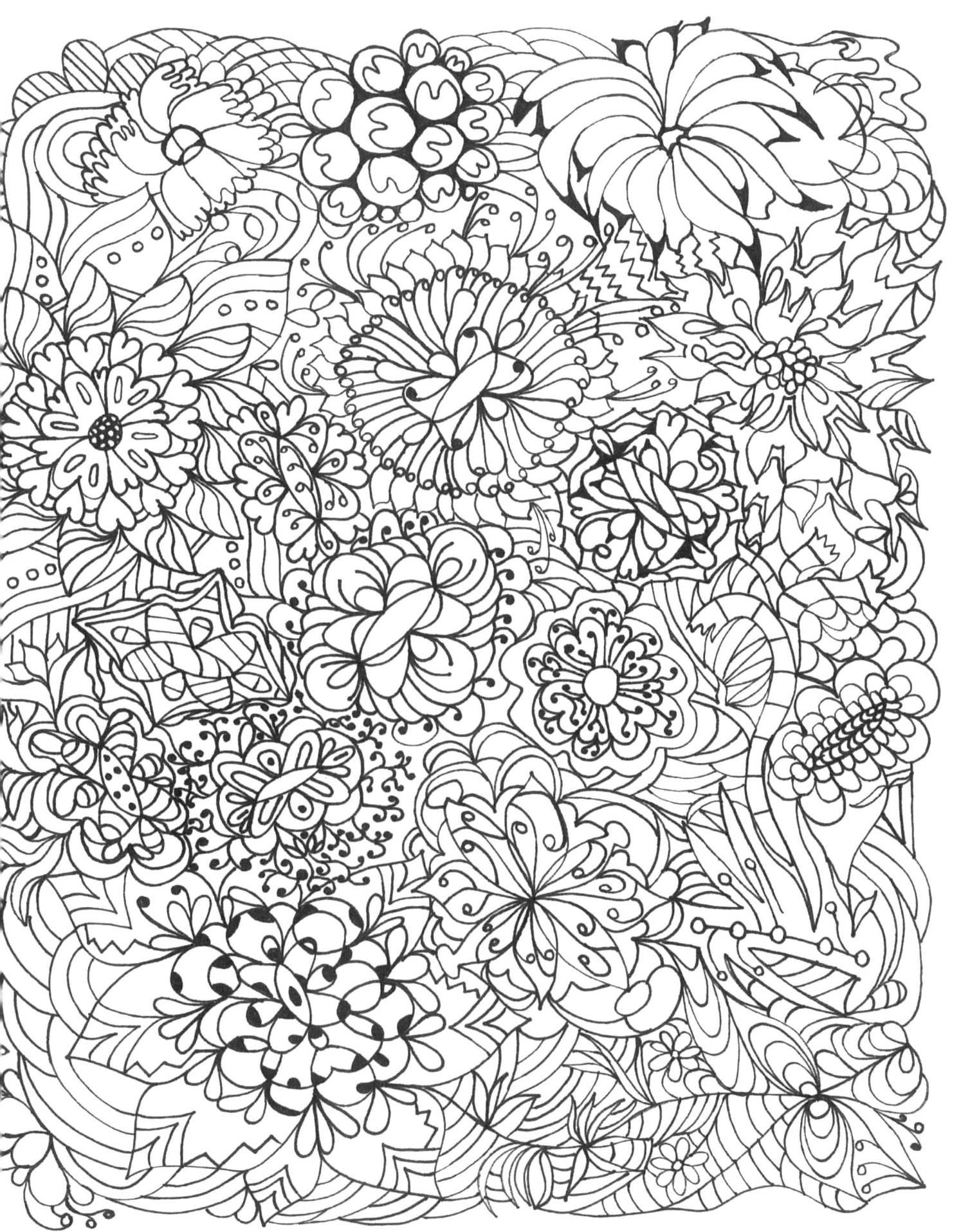

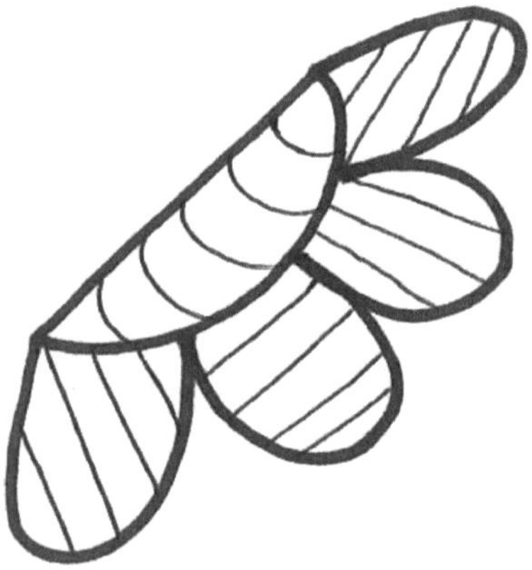

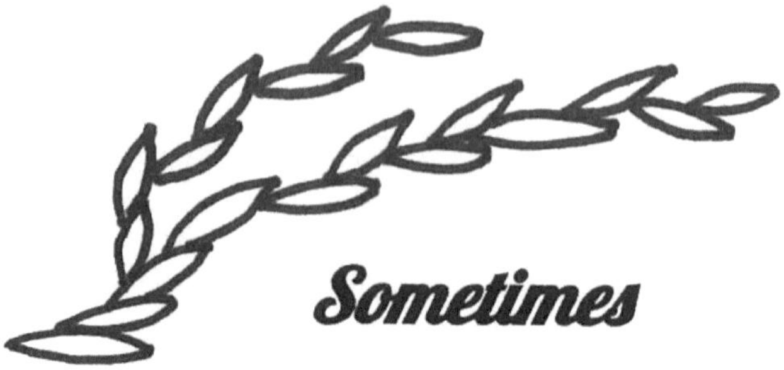

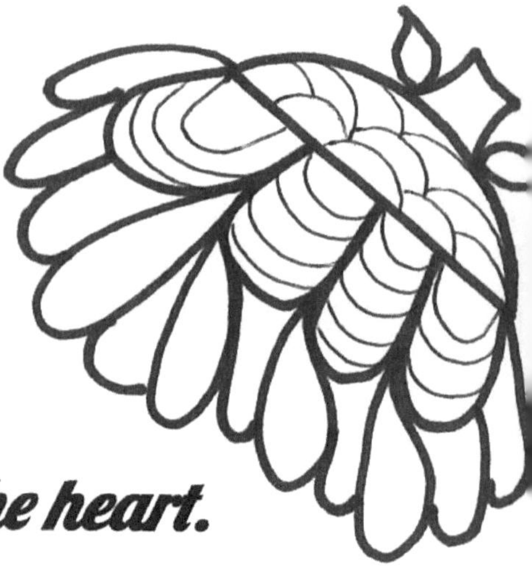

Sometimes we allow the mind to override the heart.

Stop, breathe and be present to this moment.

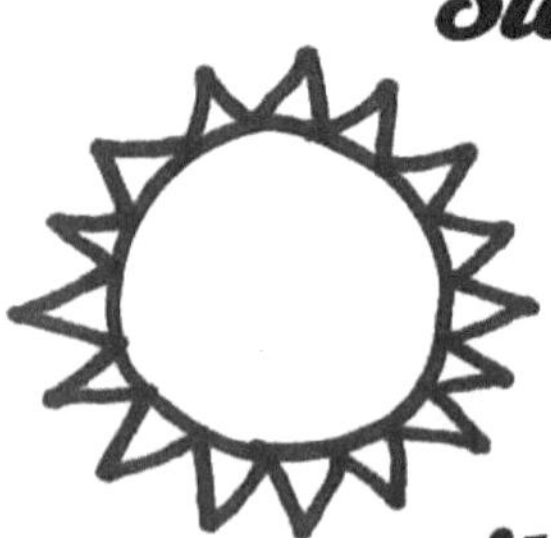

When we are present to all the positivity around us, fear, anger, and the ego are no longer in control.

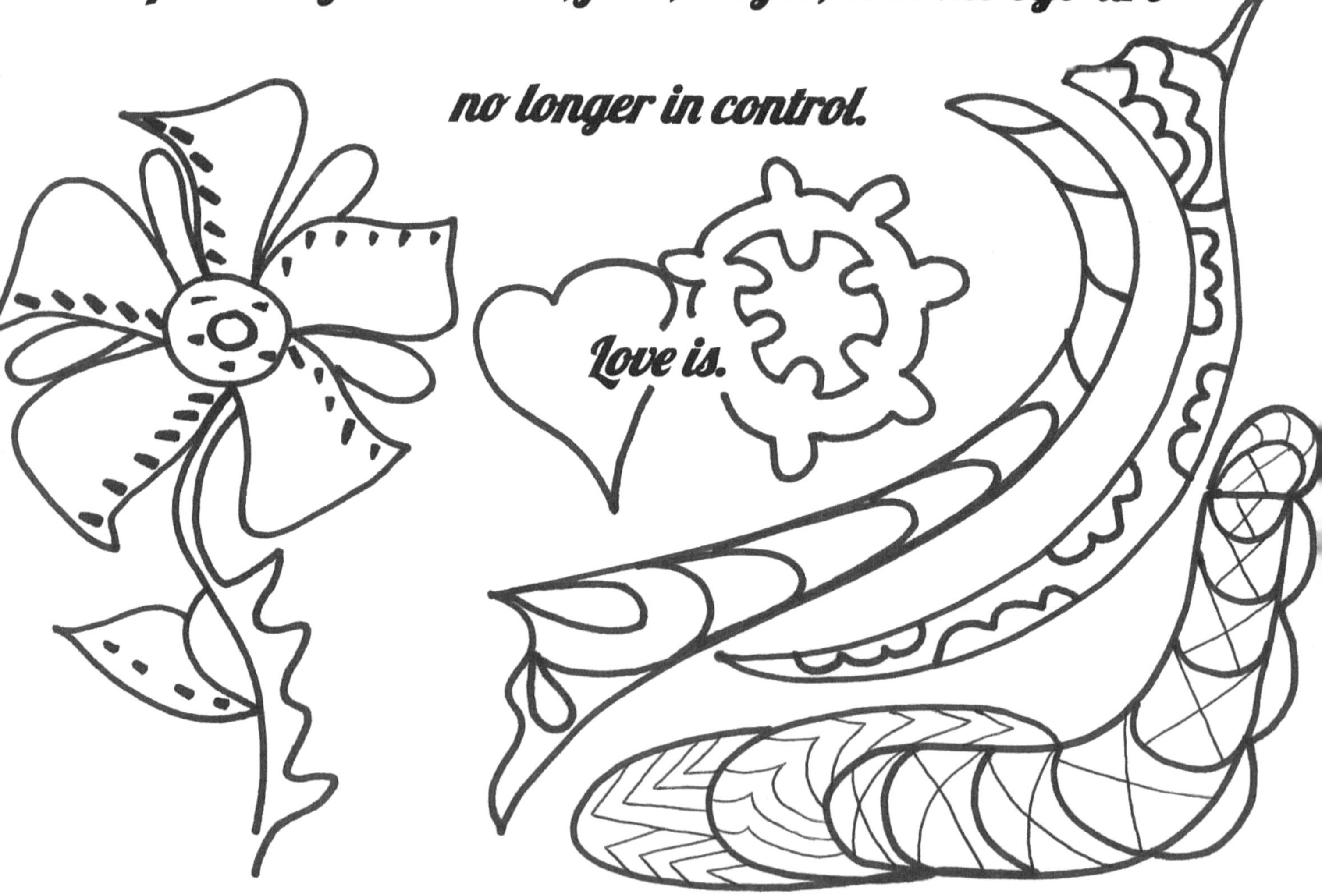

Love is.

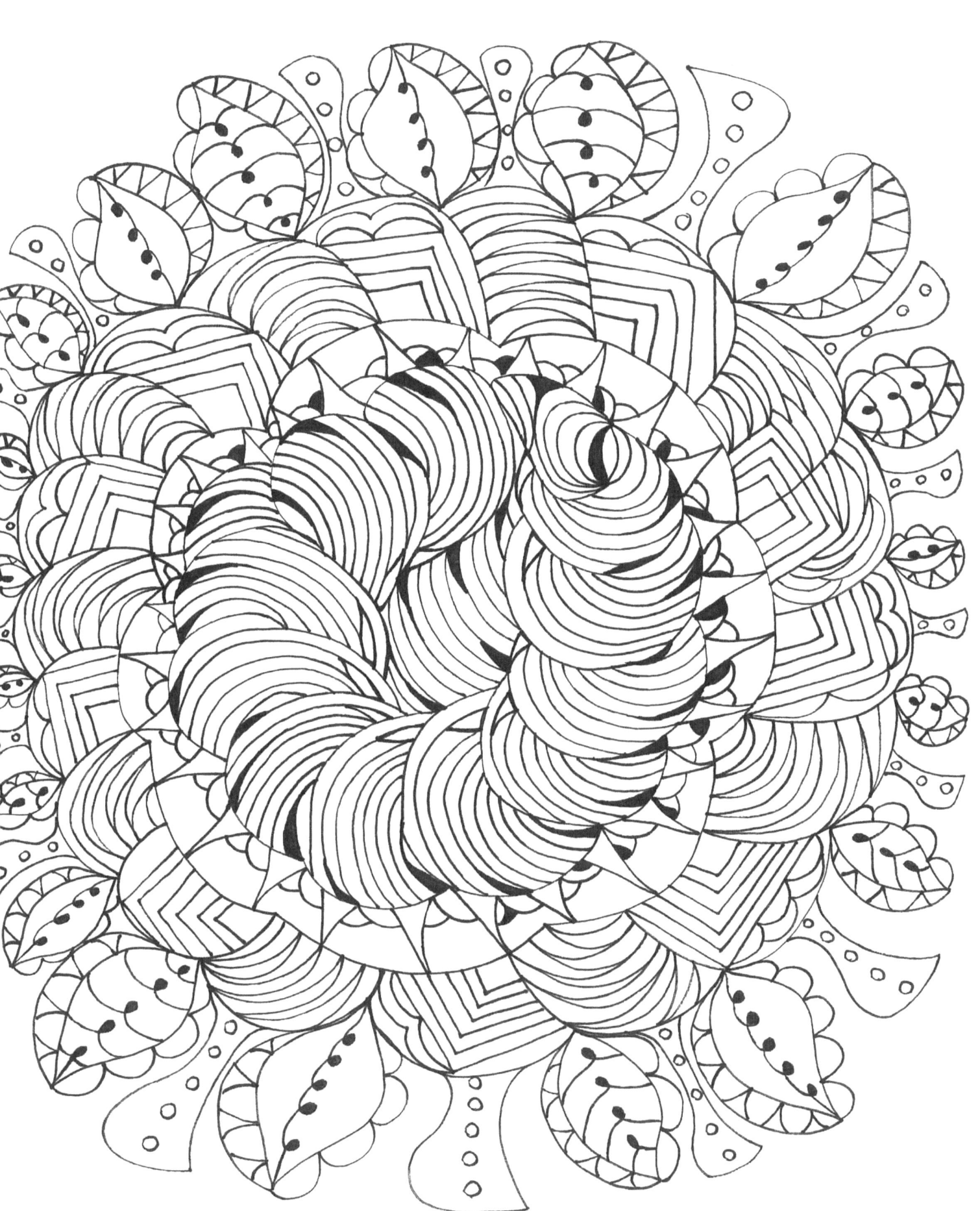

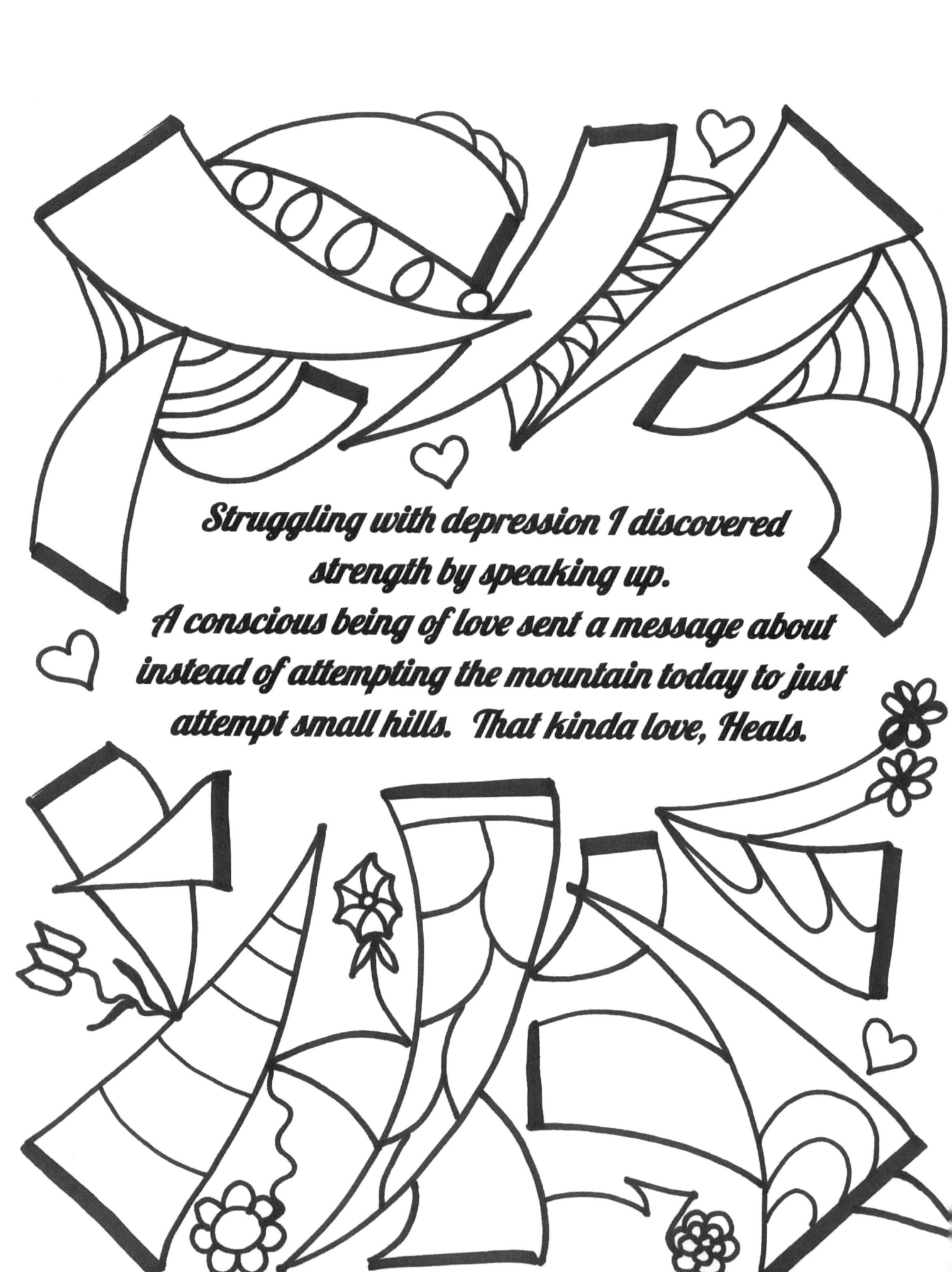

Struggling with depression I discovered strength by speaking up. A conscious being of love sent a message about instead of attempting the mountain today to just attempt small hills. That kinda love, Heals.

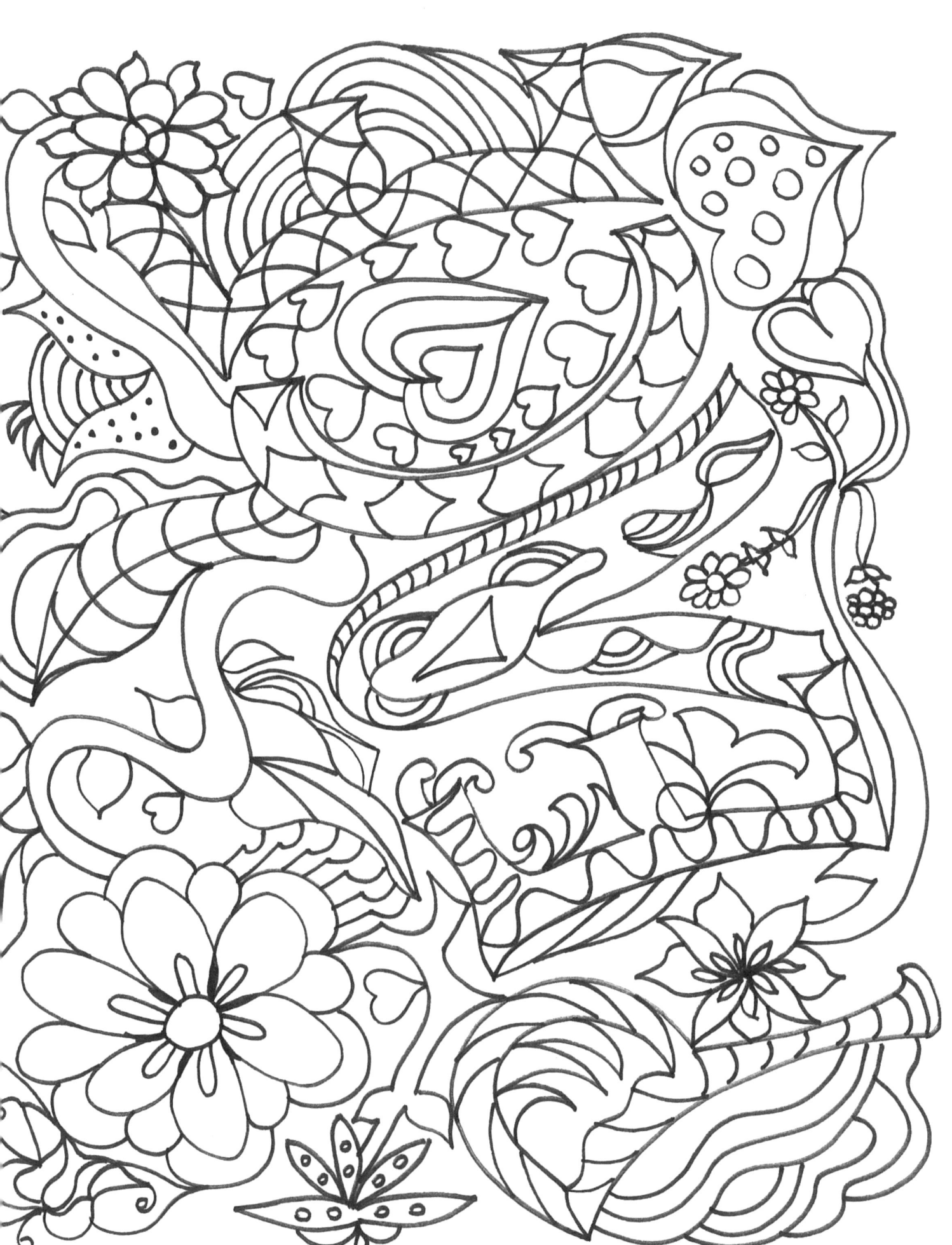

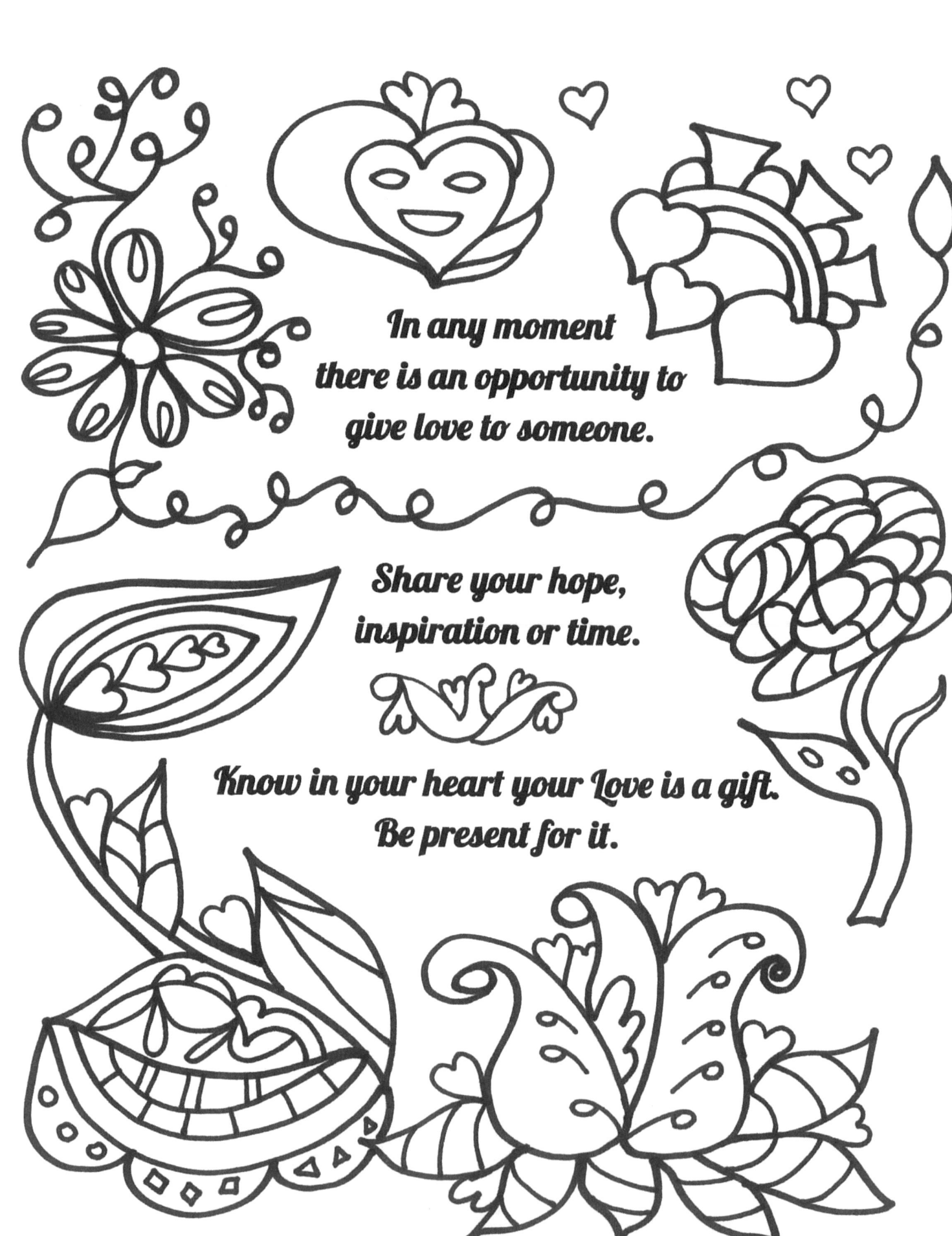

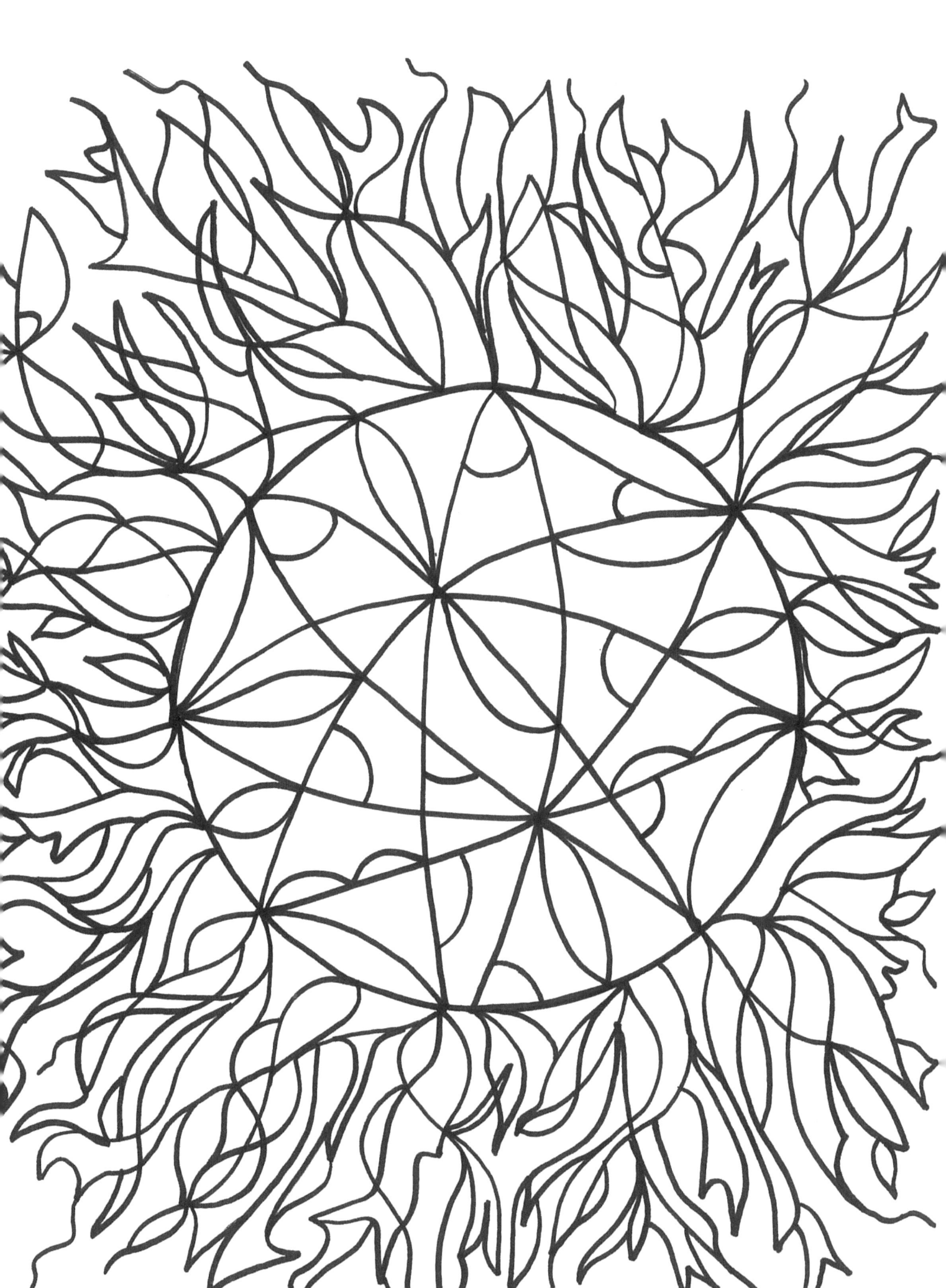

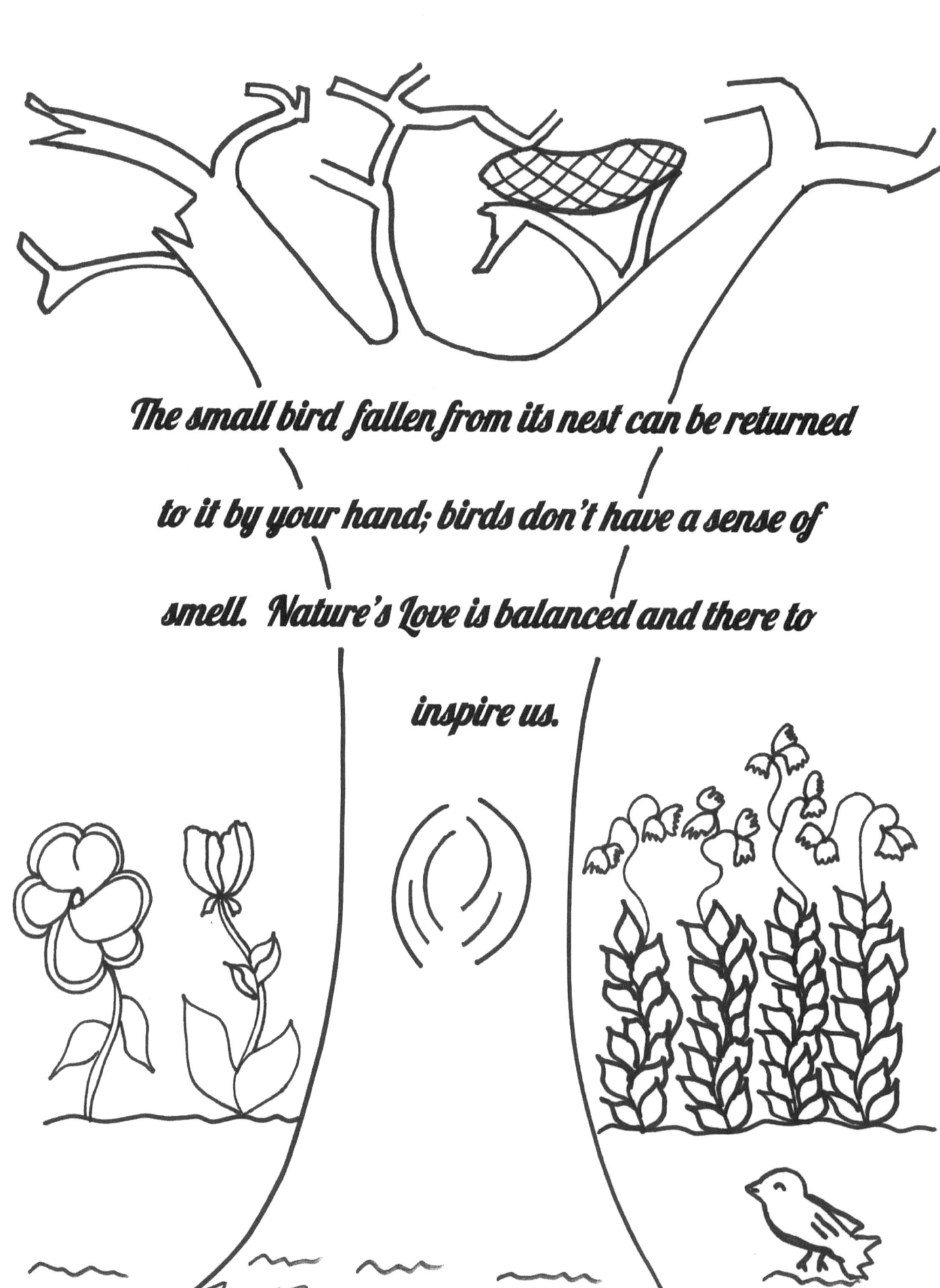

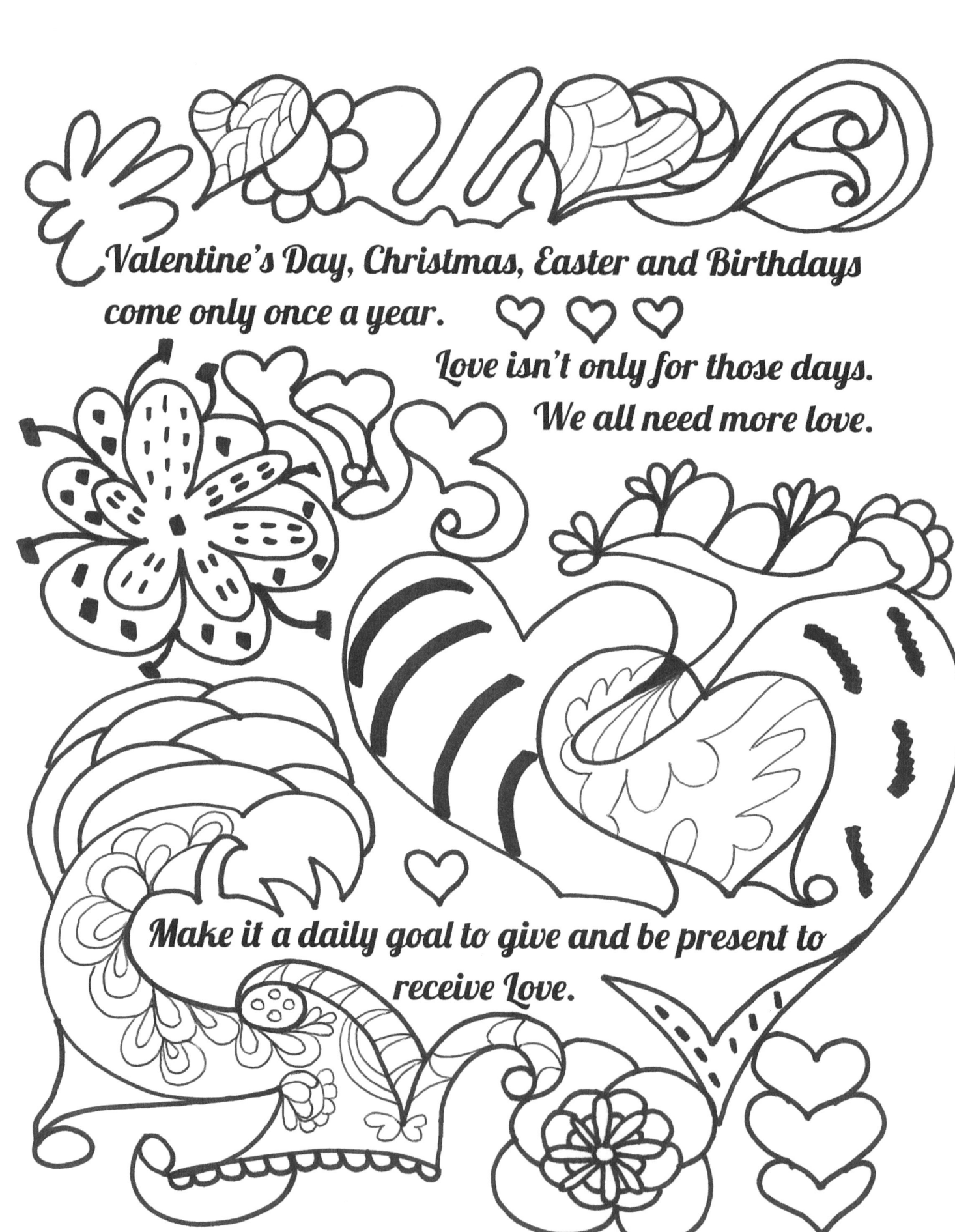

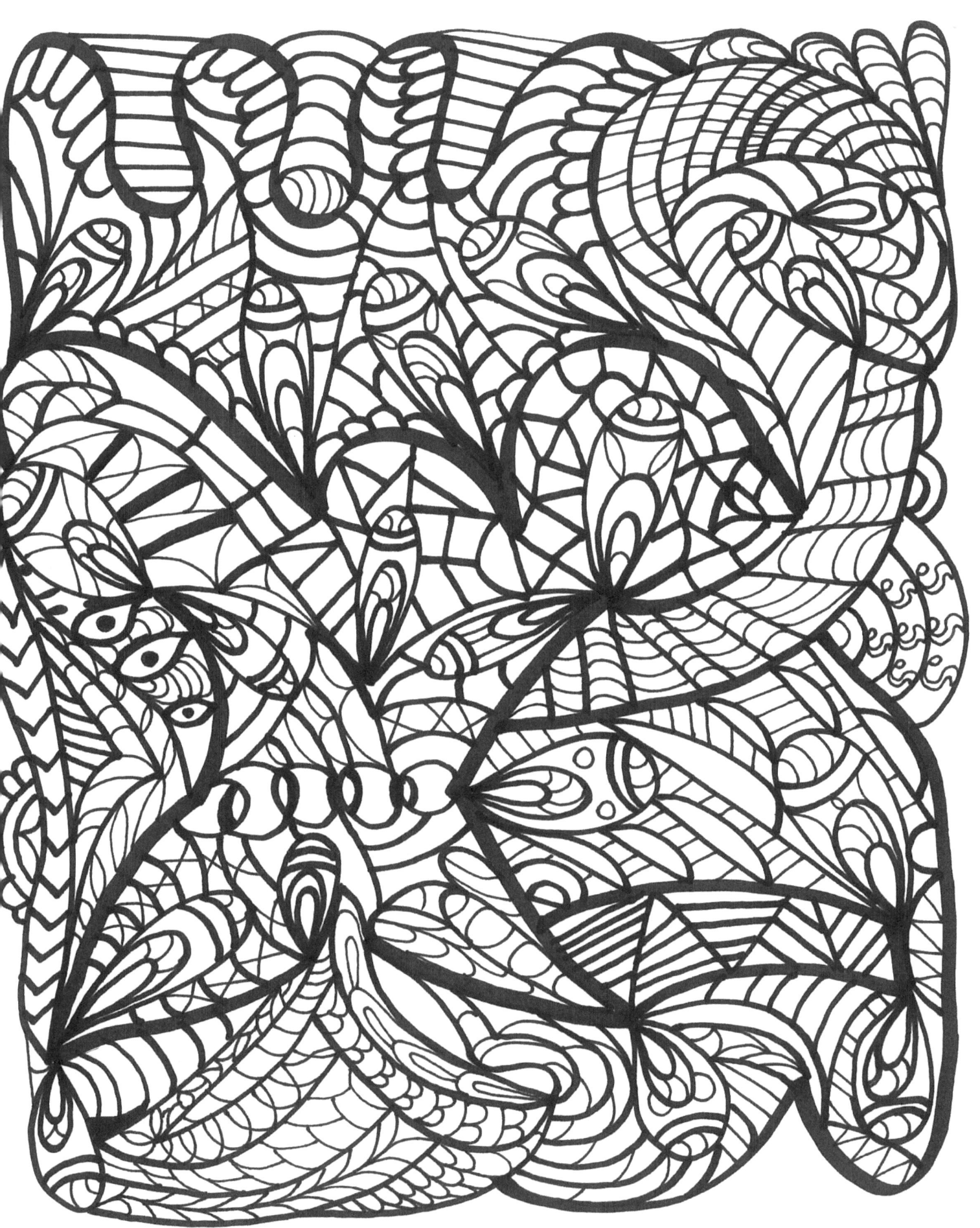

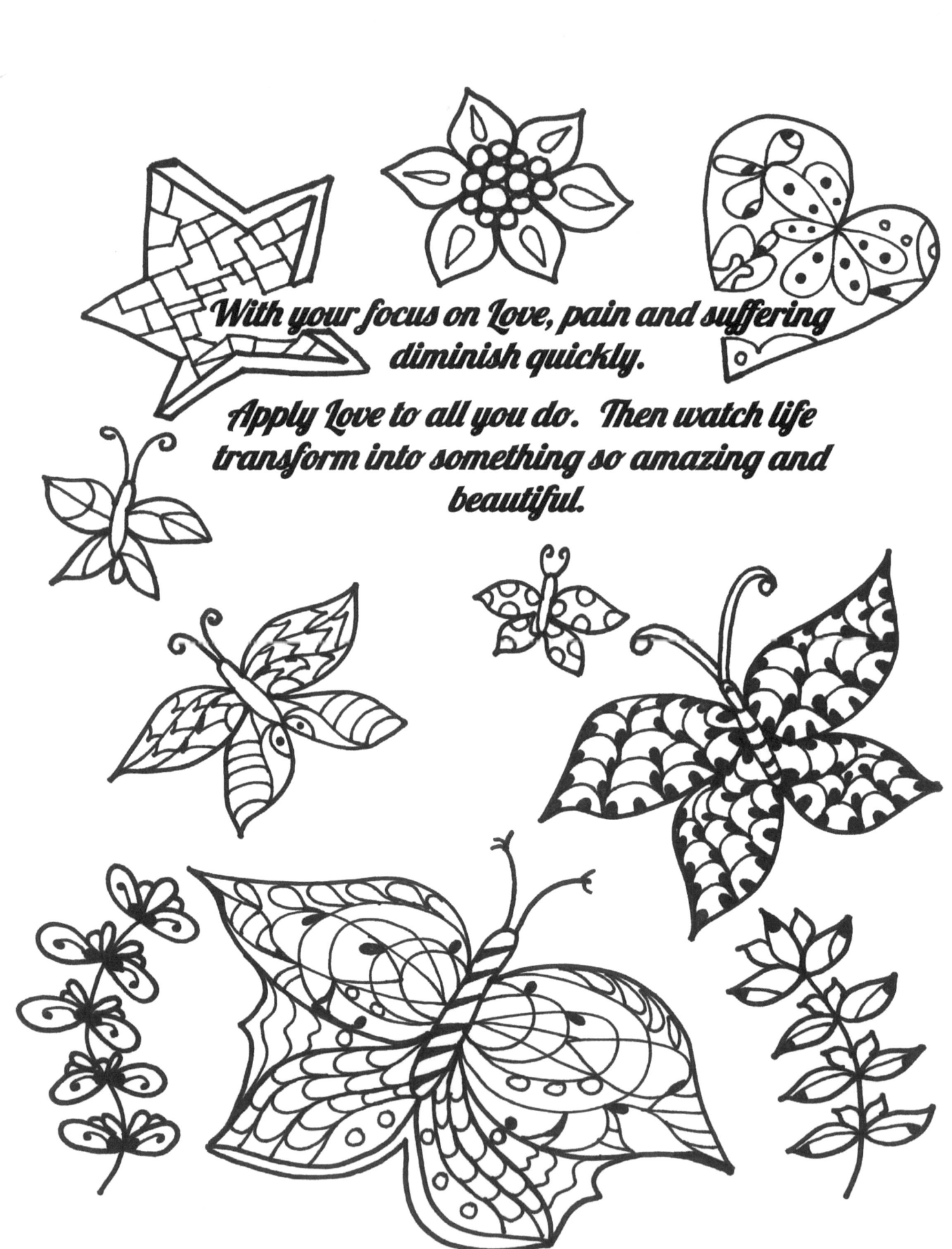

With your focus on Love, pain and suffering diminish quickly.

Apply Love to all you do. Then watch life transform into something so amazing and beautiful.

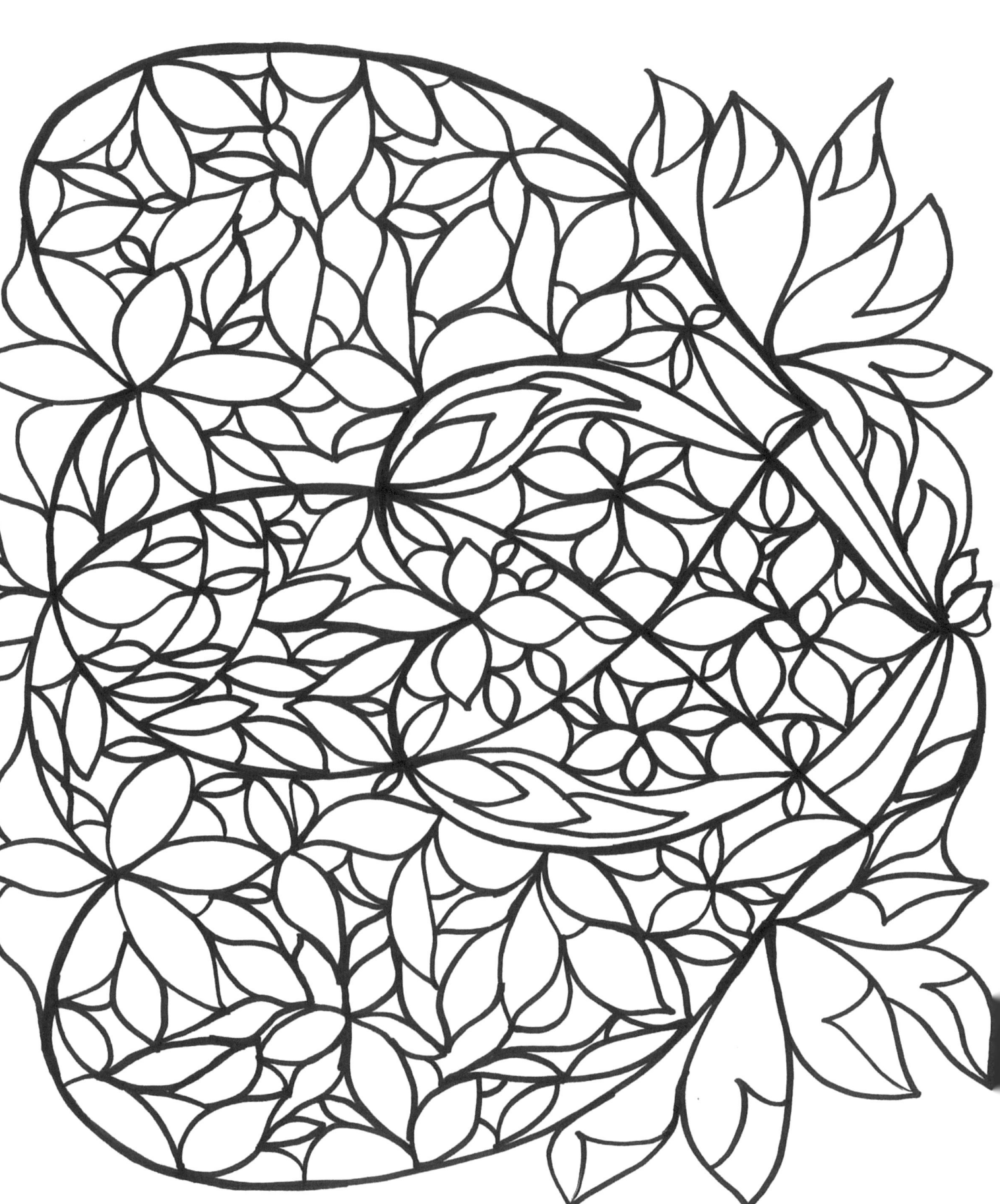

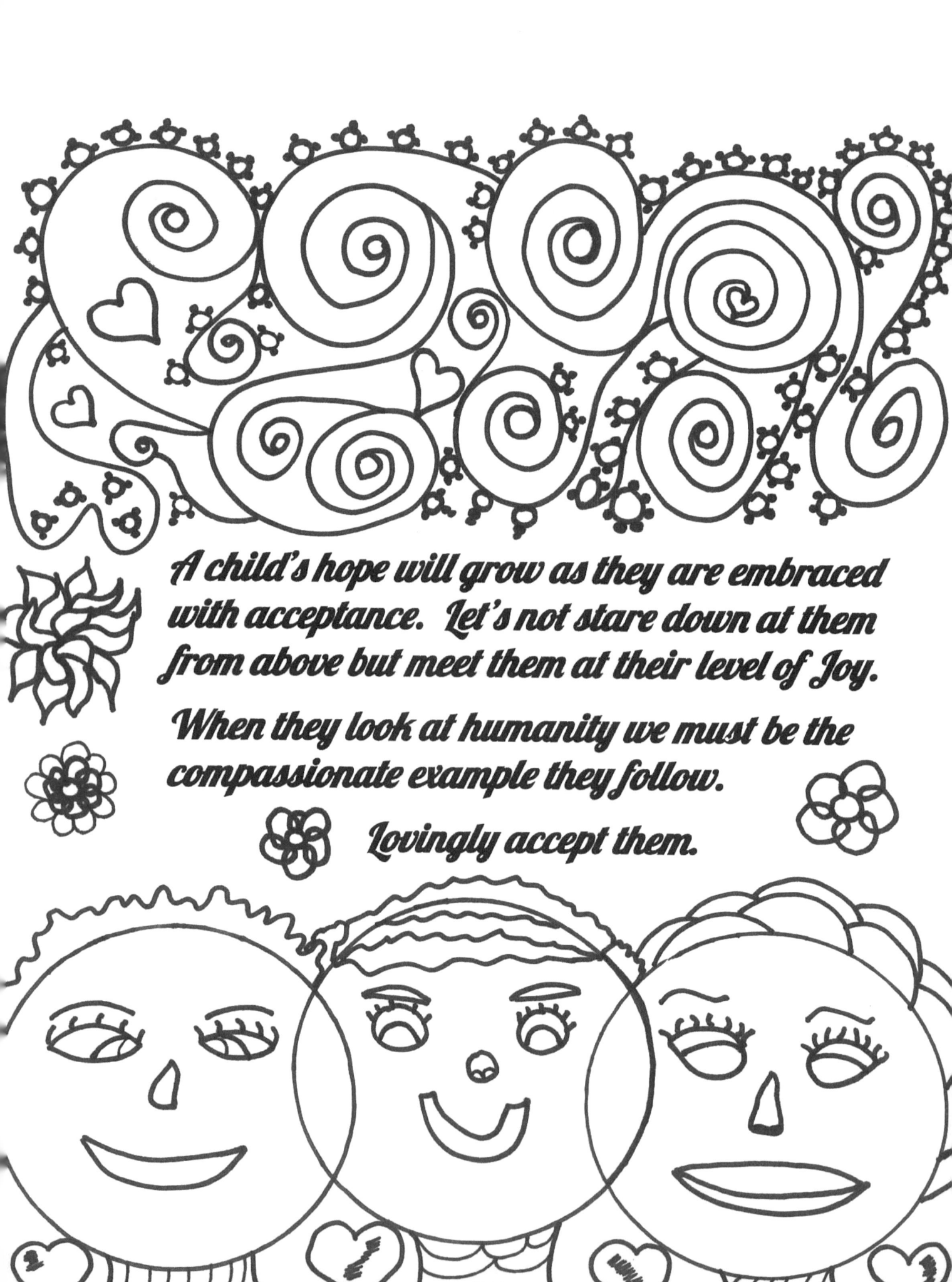

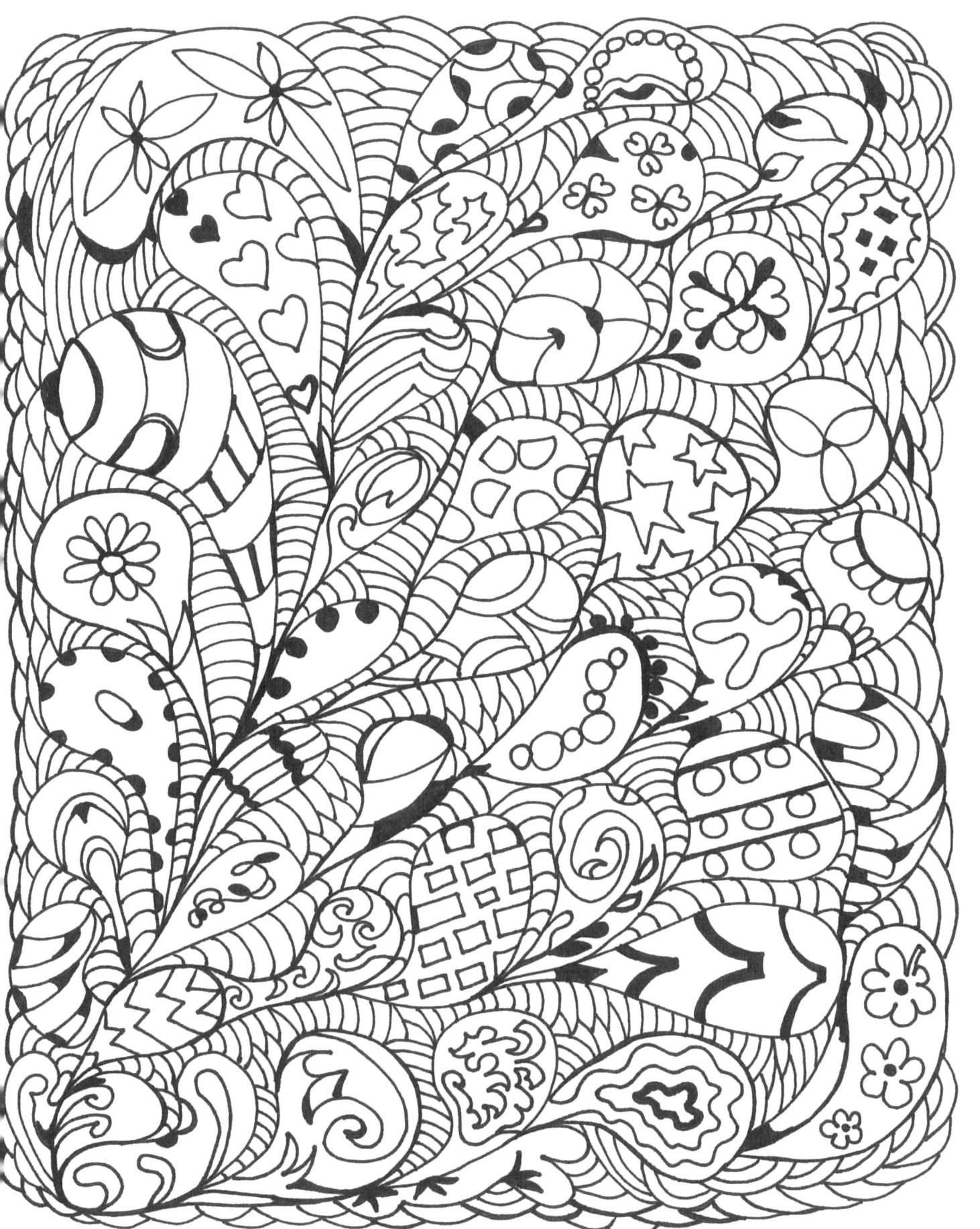

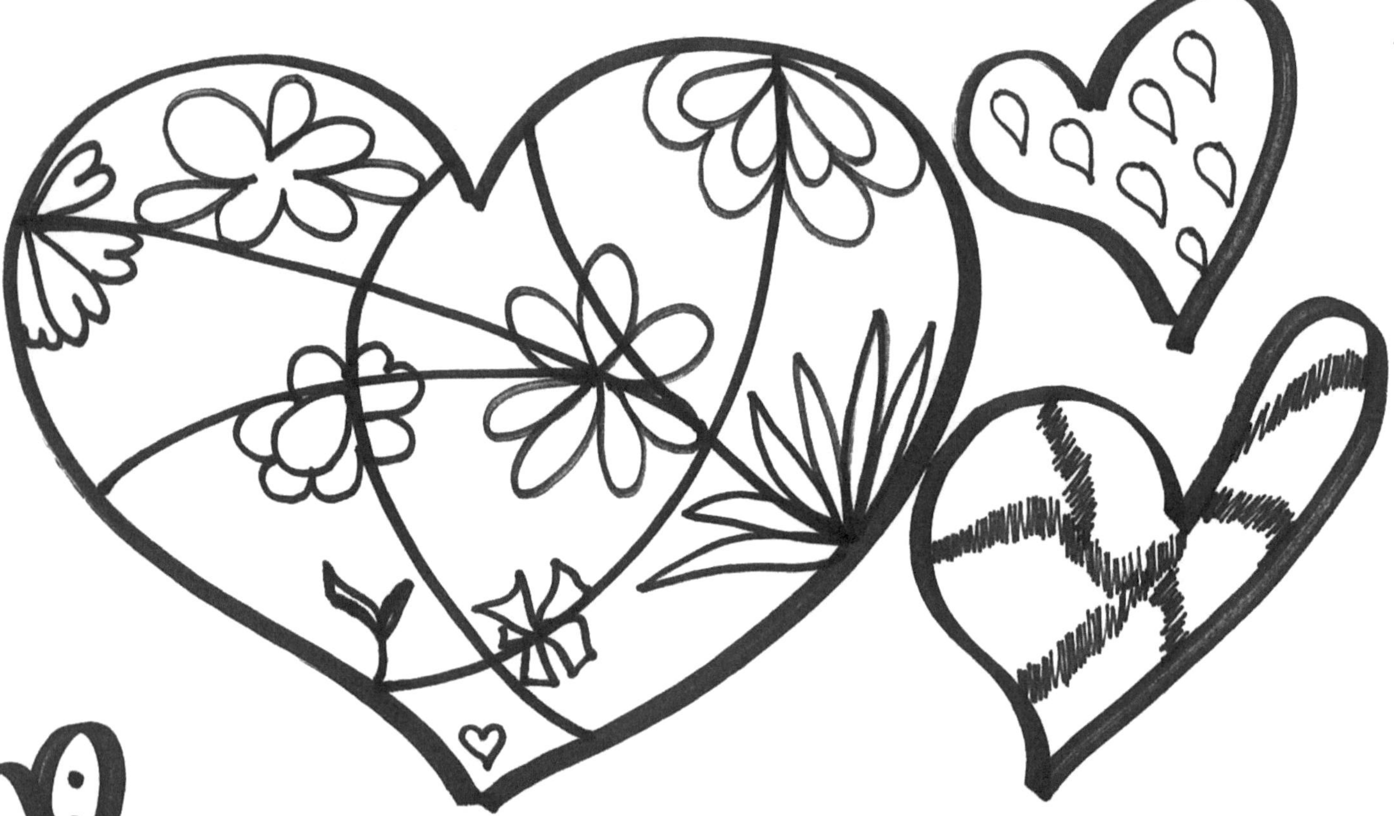

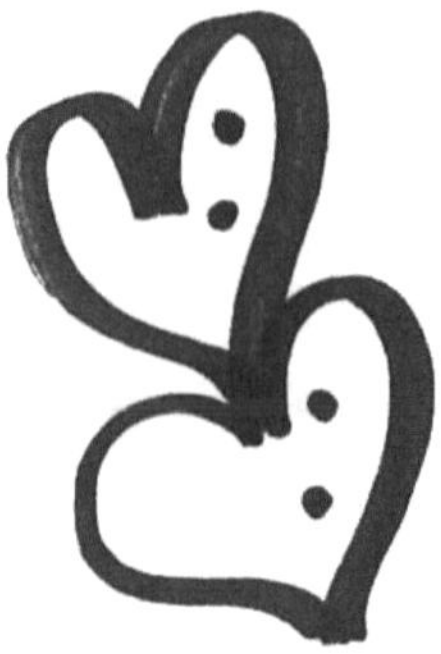

Intimate Relationships have their challenges. Authentic Love has no wants, needs or demands. Never mistake being "In Love" with Love

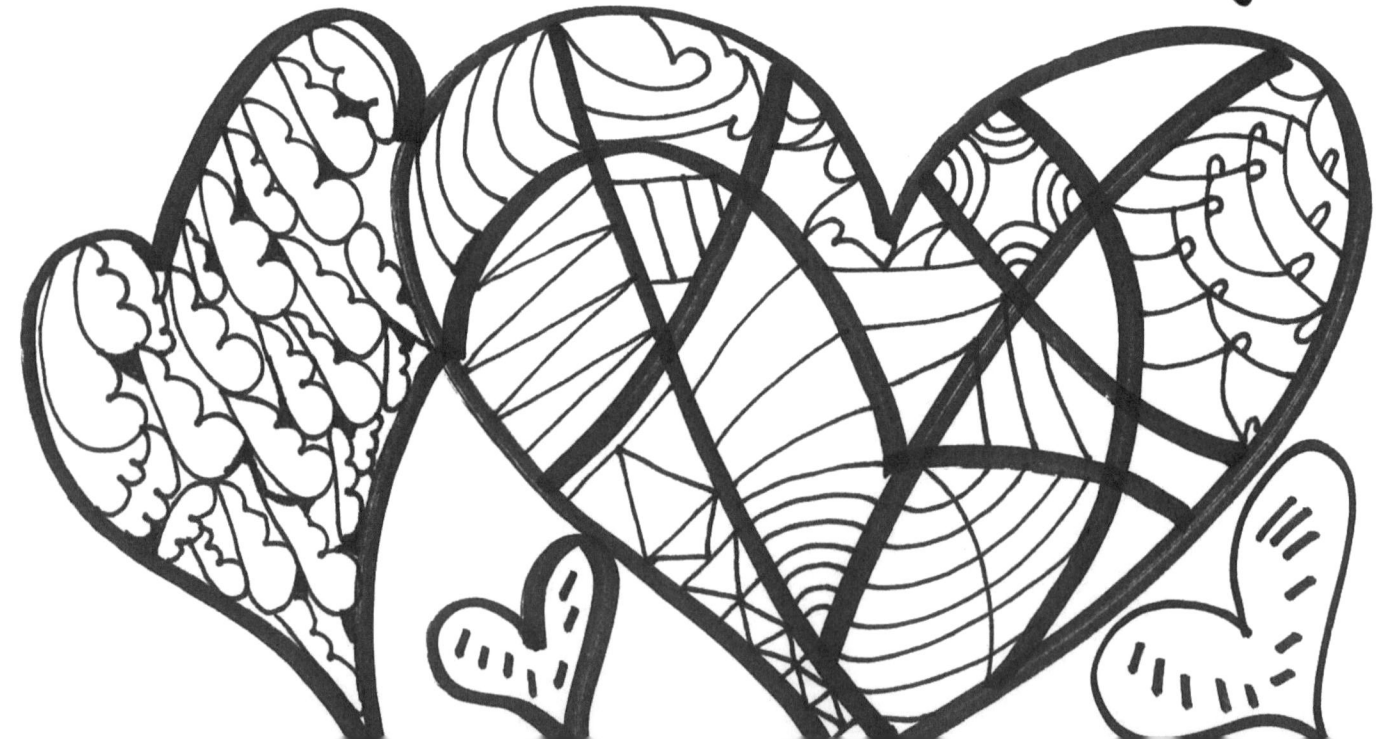

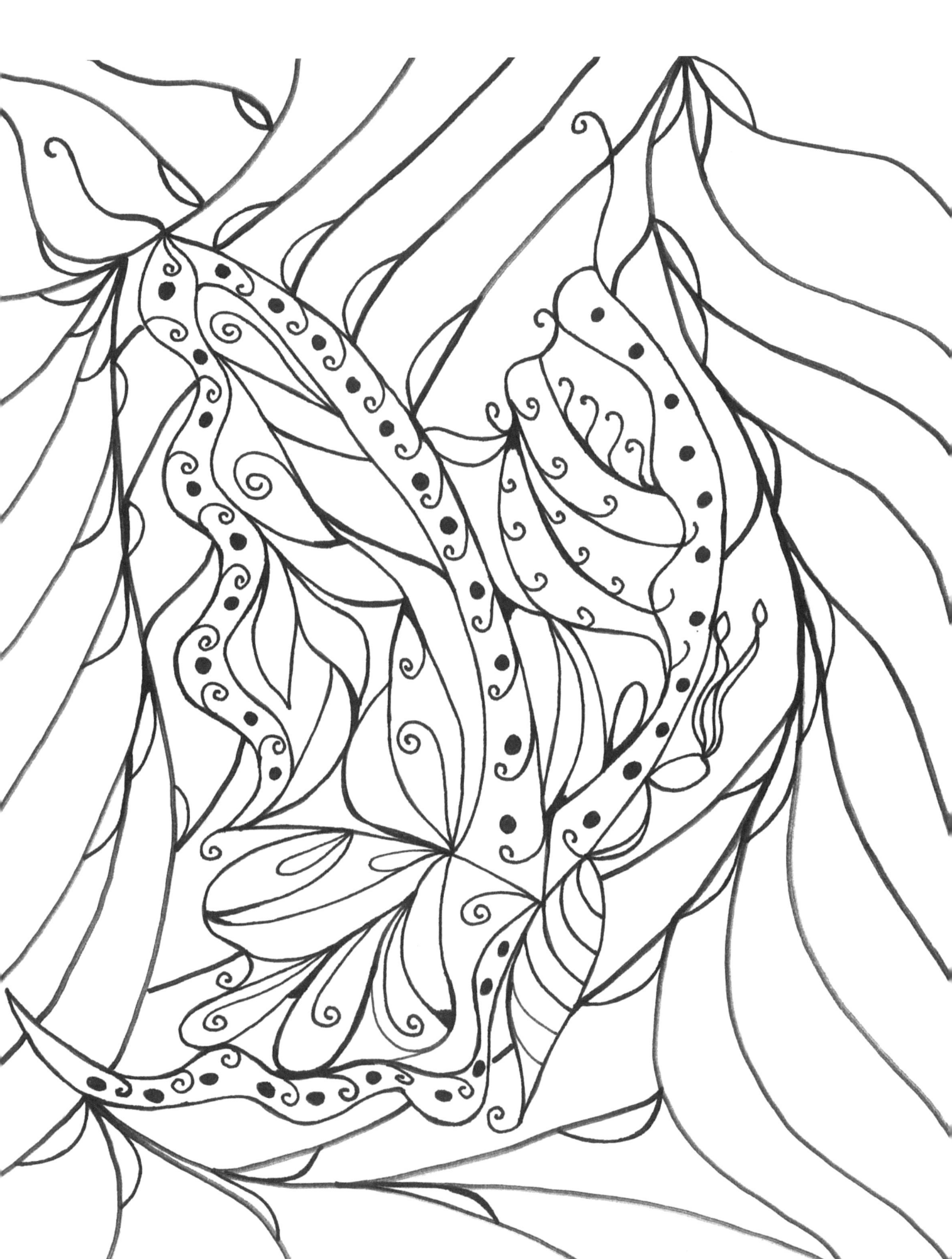

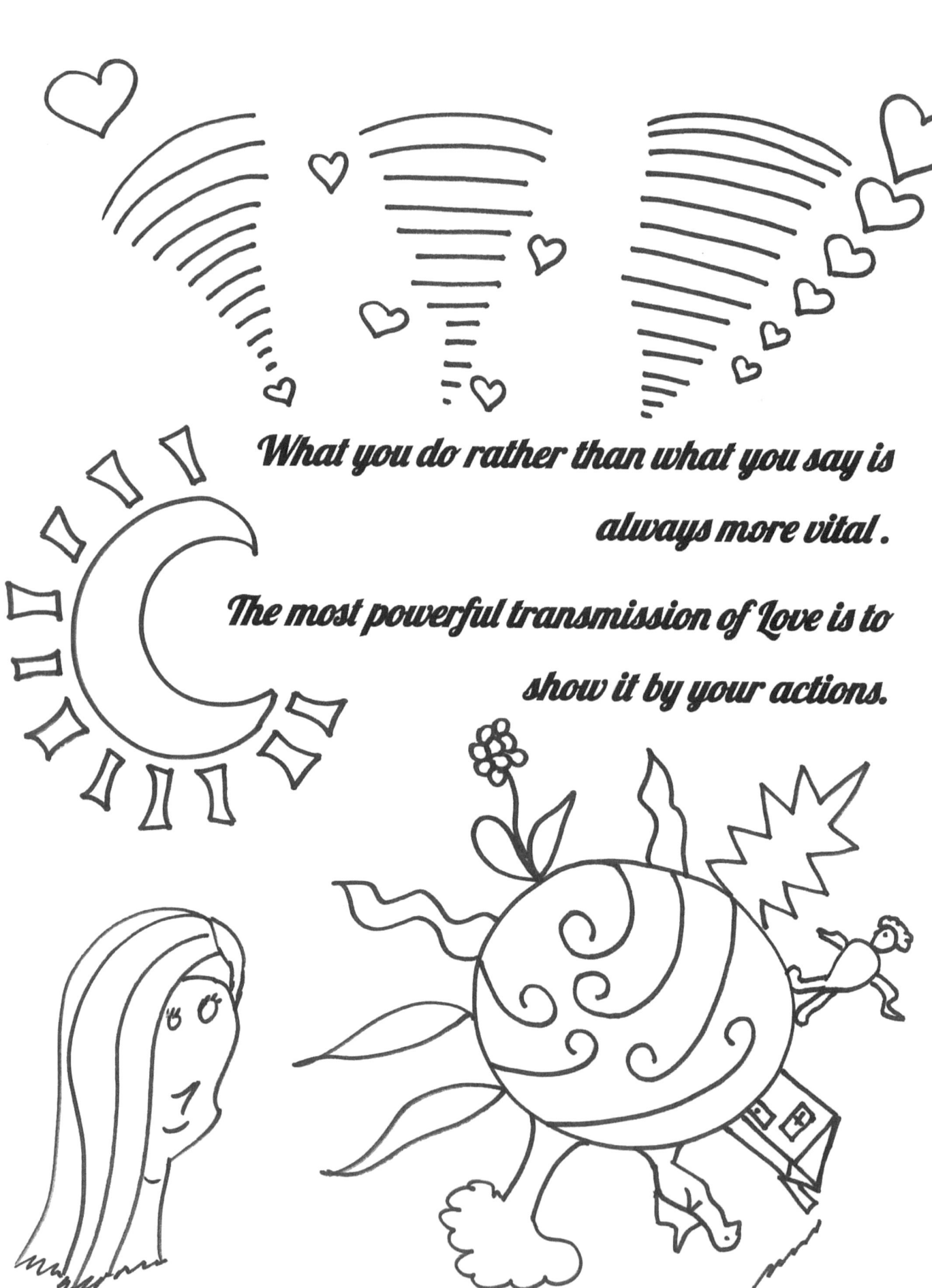

What you do rather than what you say is always more vital.

The most powerful transmission of Love is to show it by your actions.

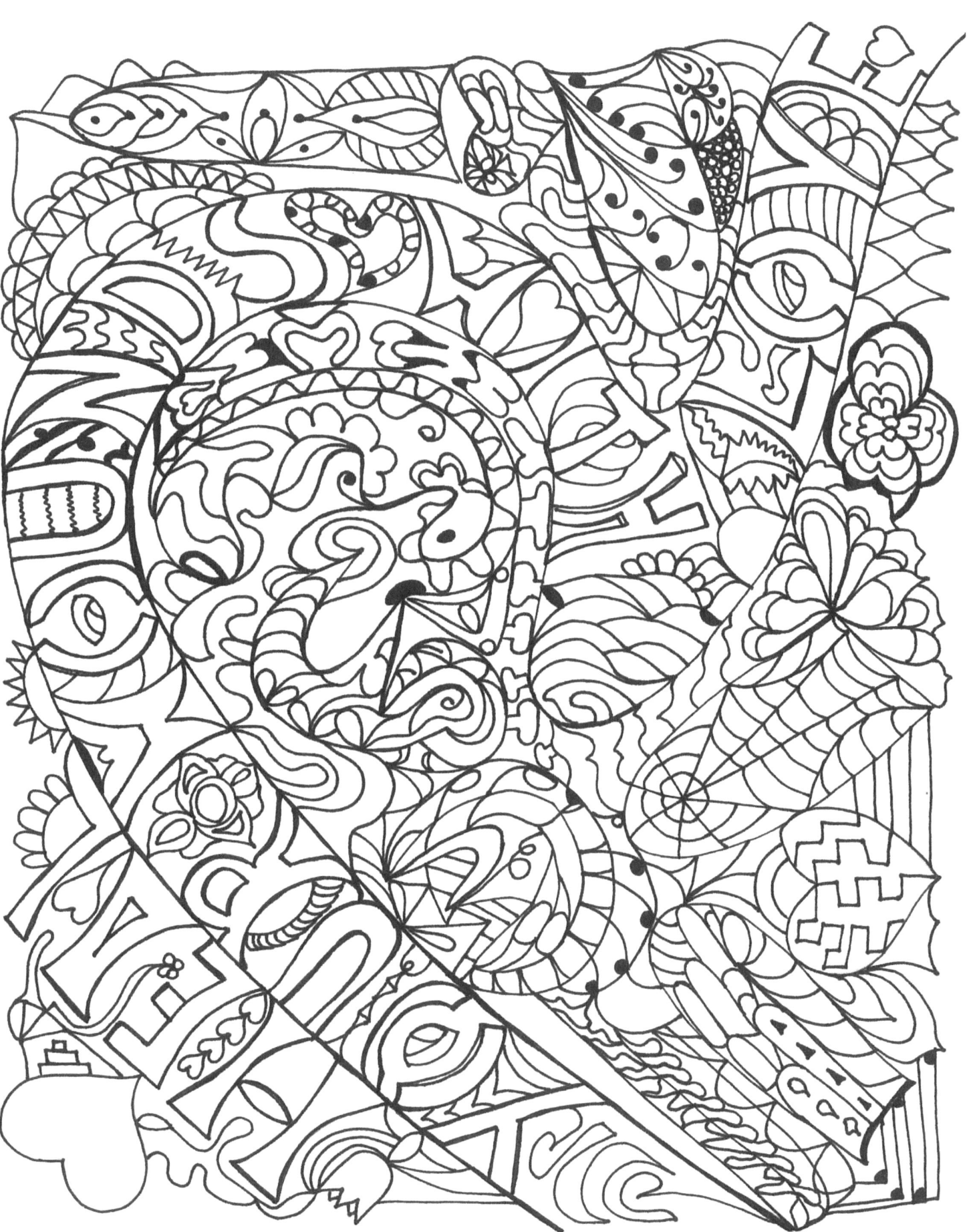

When you need Love where can you find it?

Love is abundant in Nature. We are Nature and all we have to do is be present to observe it.

Look for it in your pet's, partner's or friend's eyes.

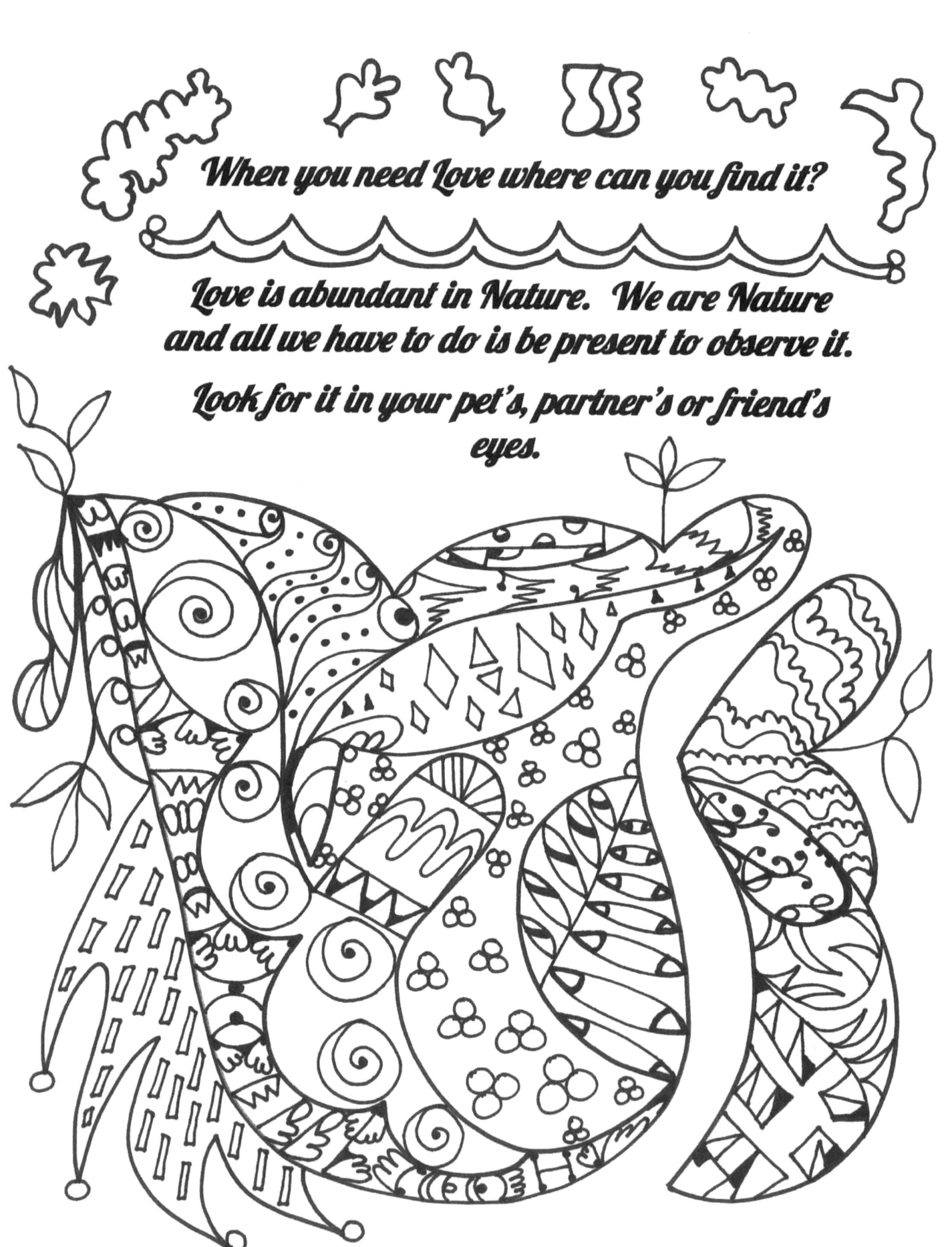

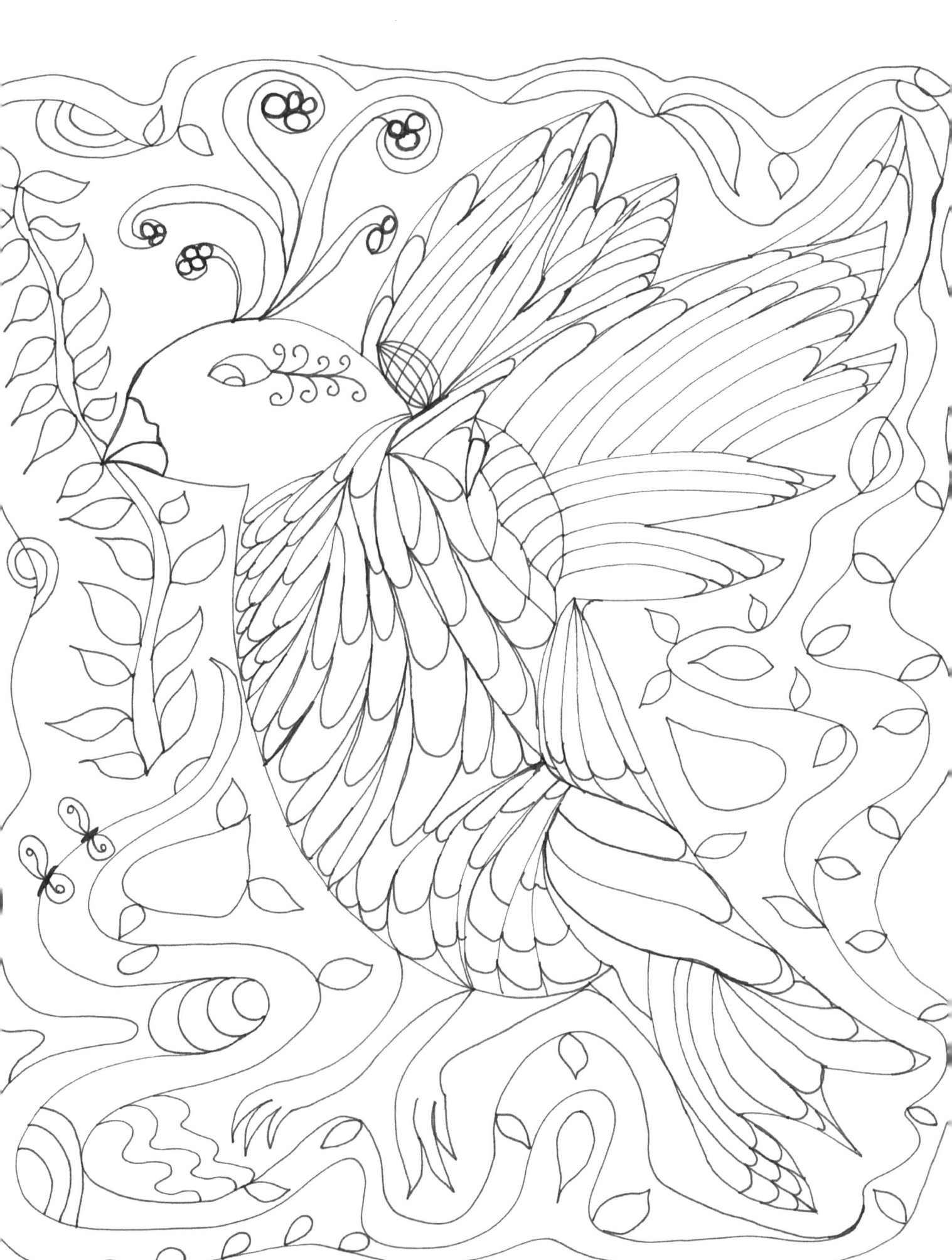

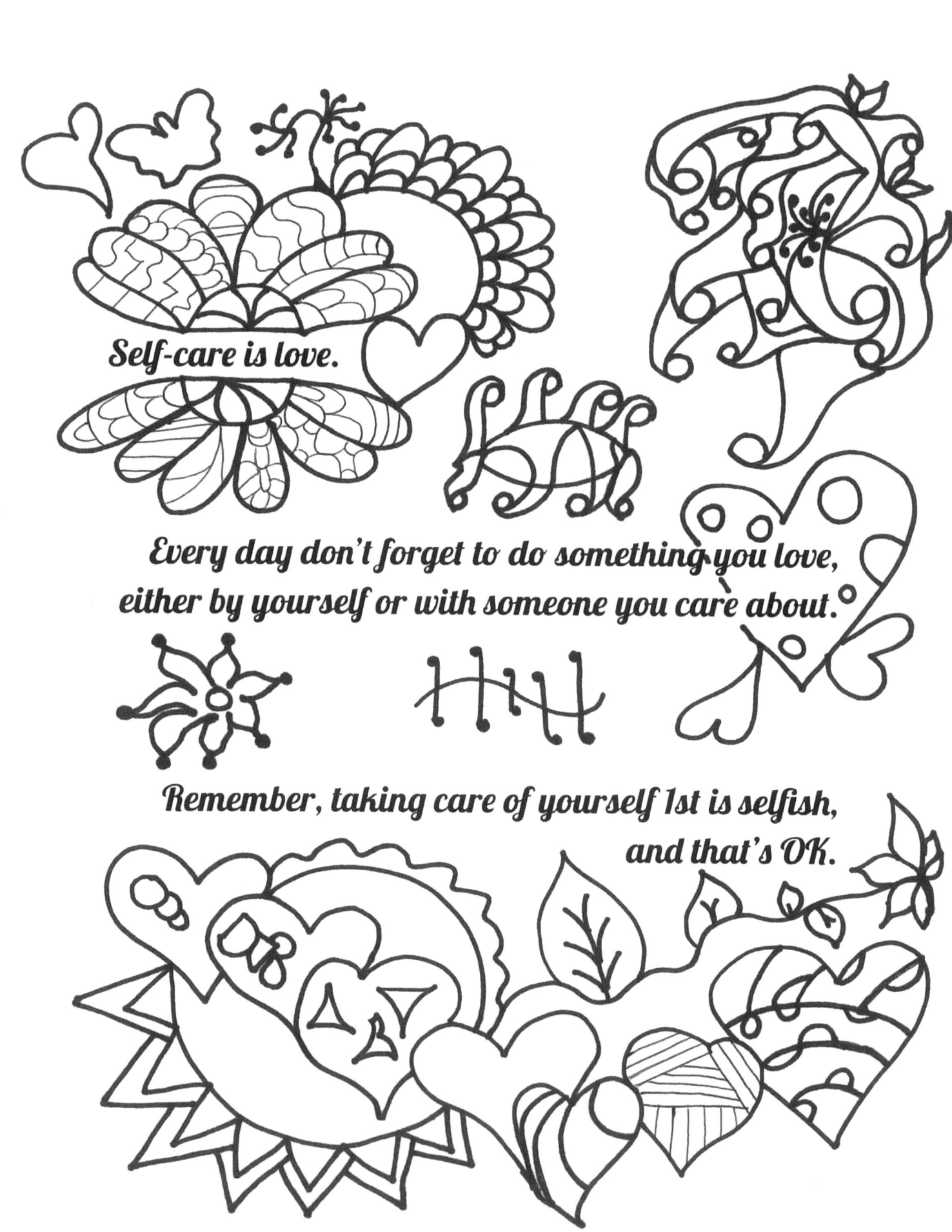

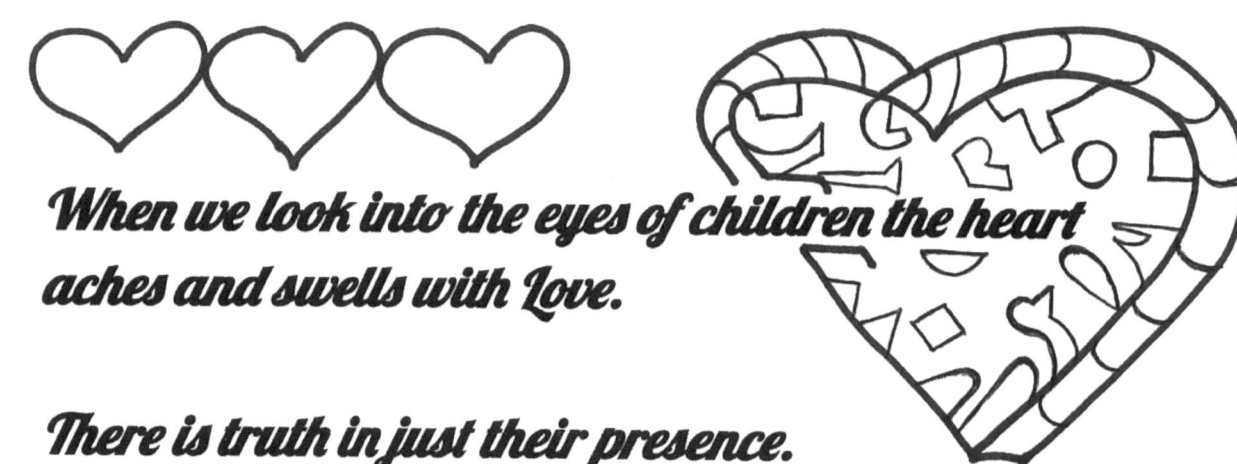

When we look into the eyes of children the heart aches and swells with Love.

There is truth in just their presence.

Experience life through their eyes and learn just how special Love really is.

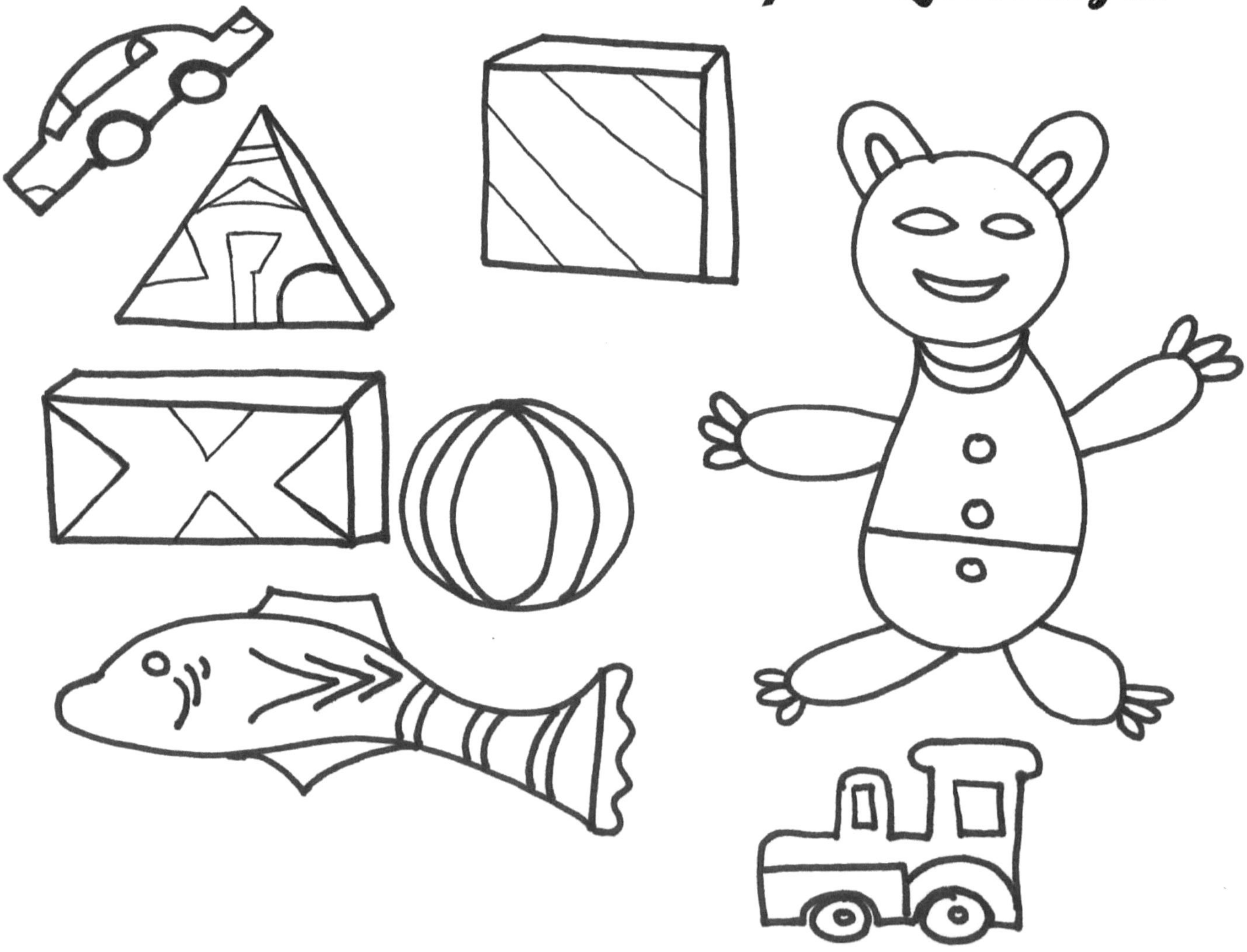

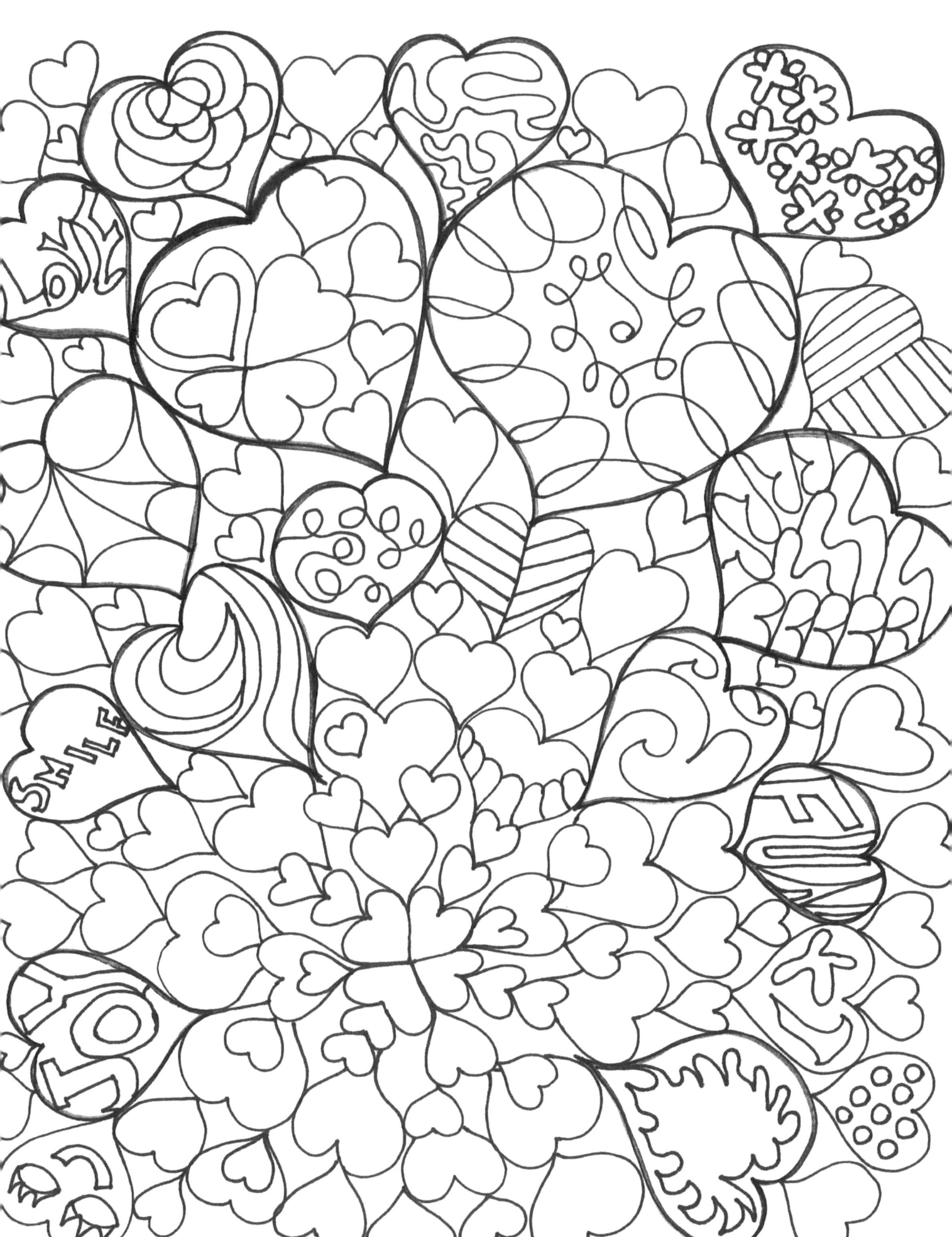

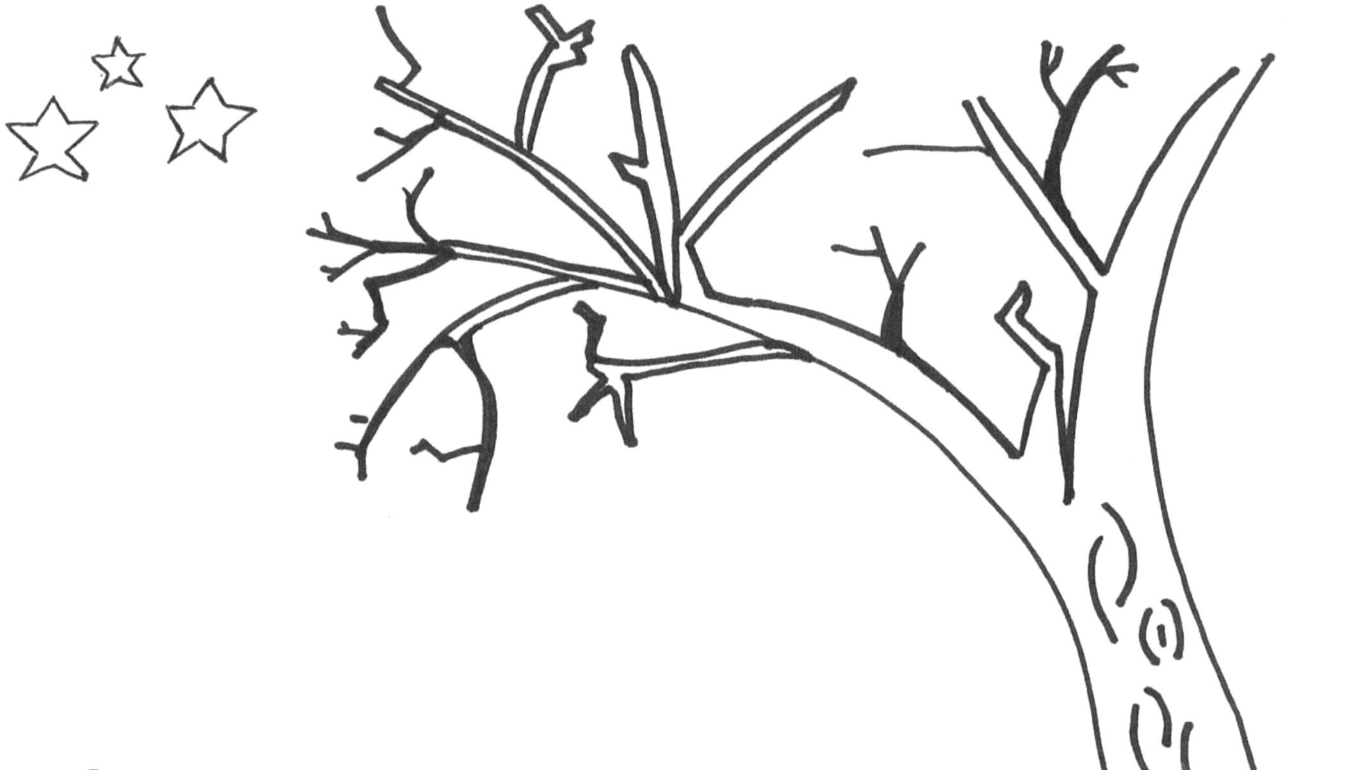

Lie in the grass, enjoy the sun on your face. Stare up at the night sky, marvel at the glorious space of infinity.

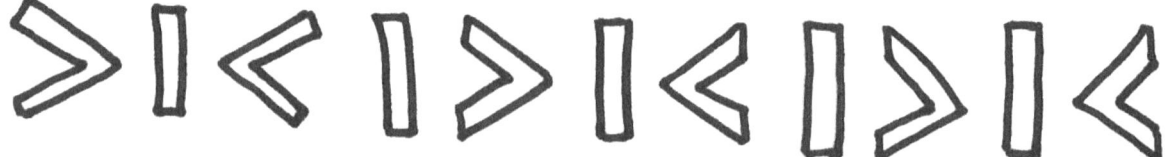

When you are conscious of love, everything has light, from the sun to the stars and beyond.

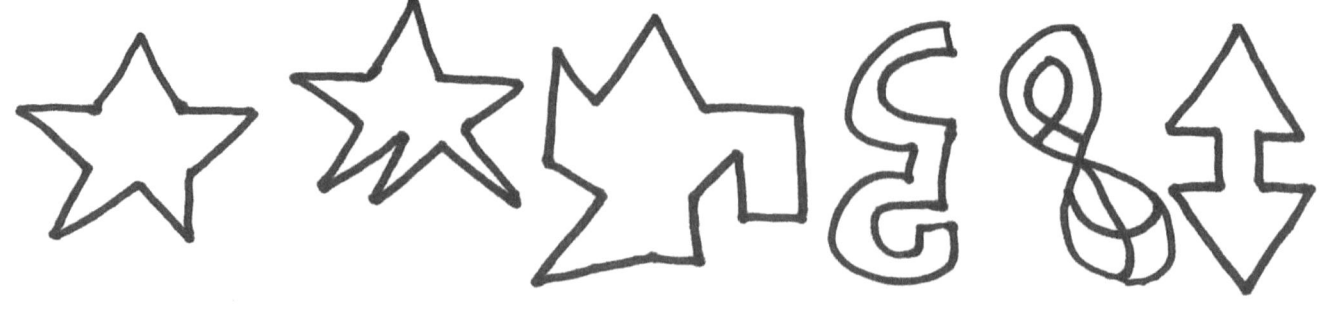

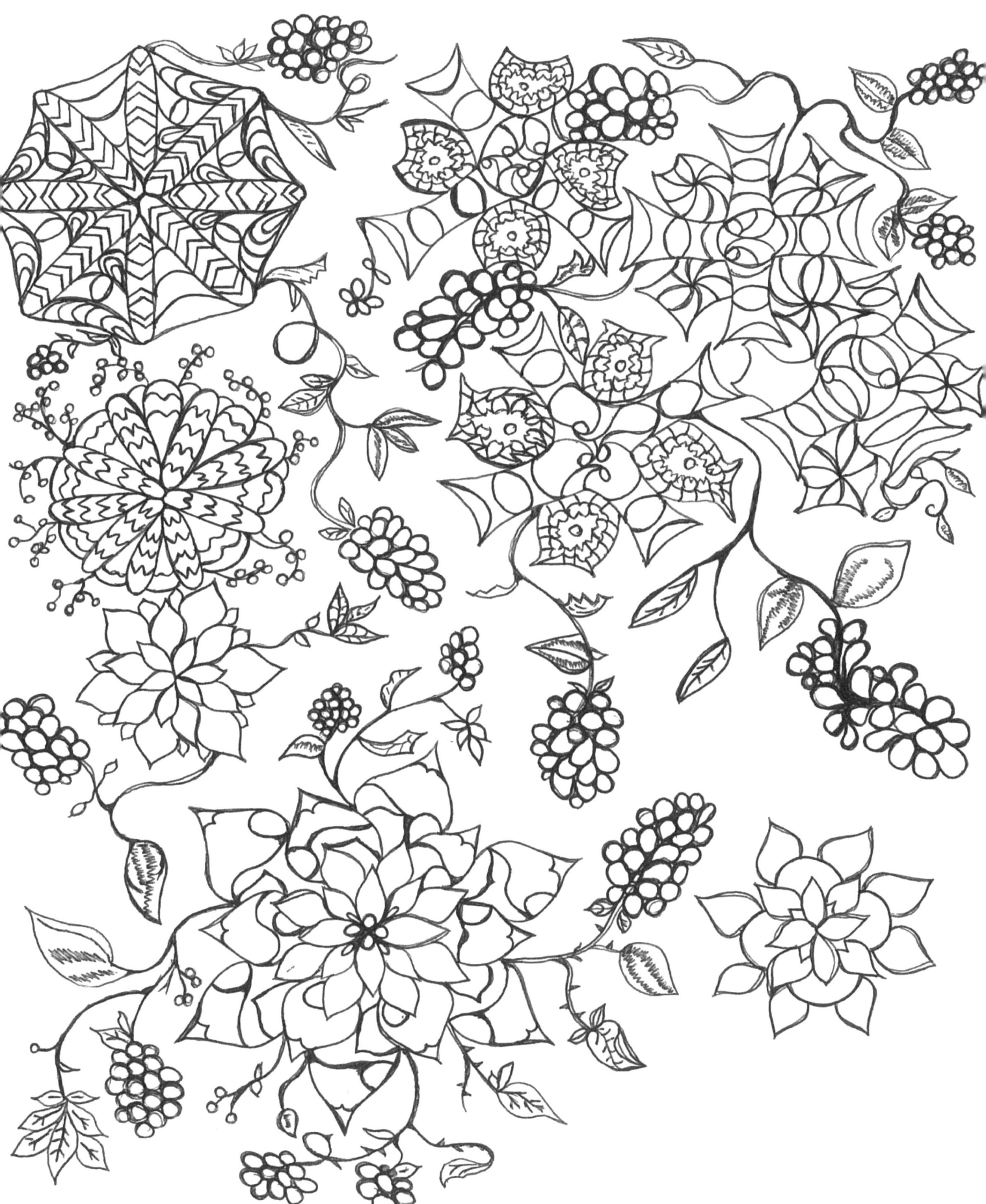

When the soul and heart are open that allows the truth to shine in.

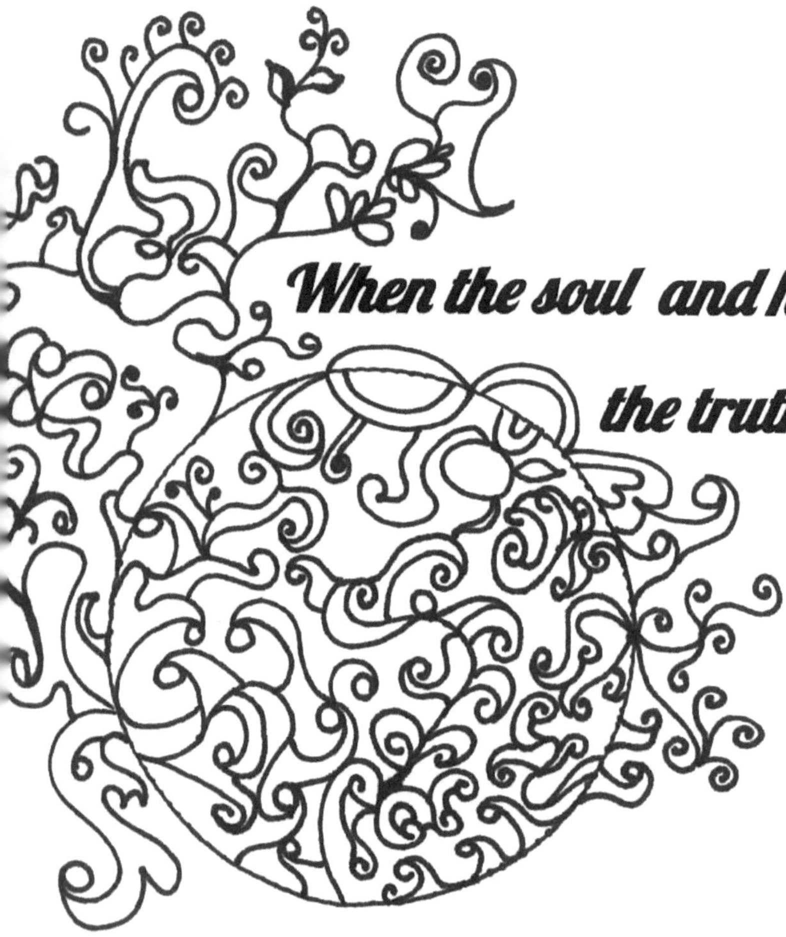

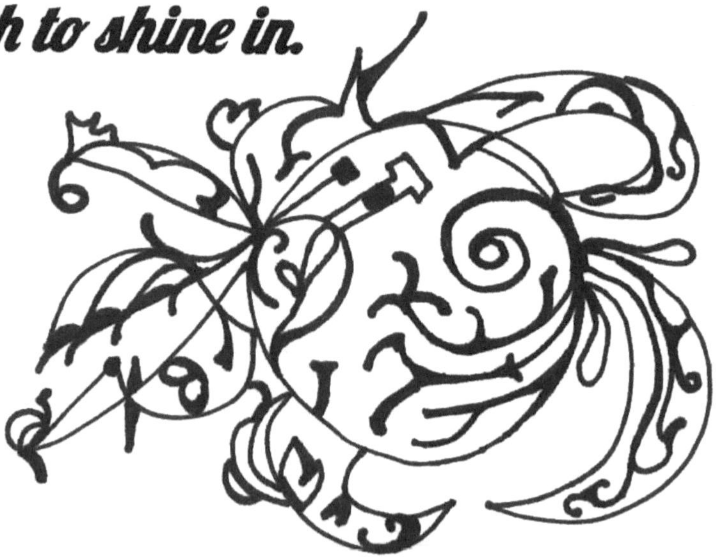

Release the bondages of the past and the worries of the future.

Be present every day for Love is the Truth.

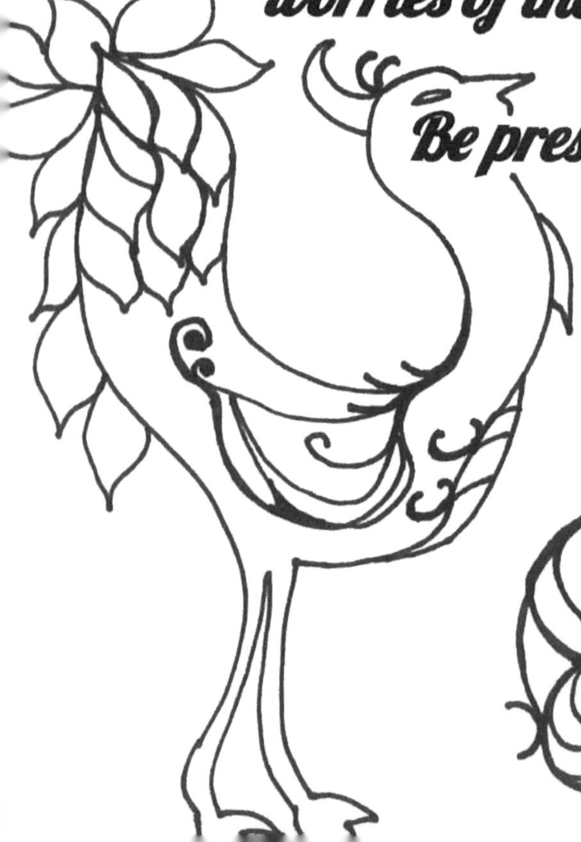

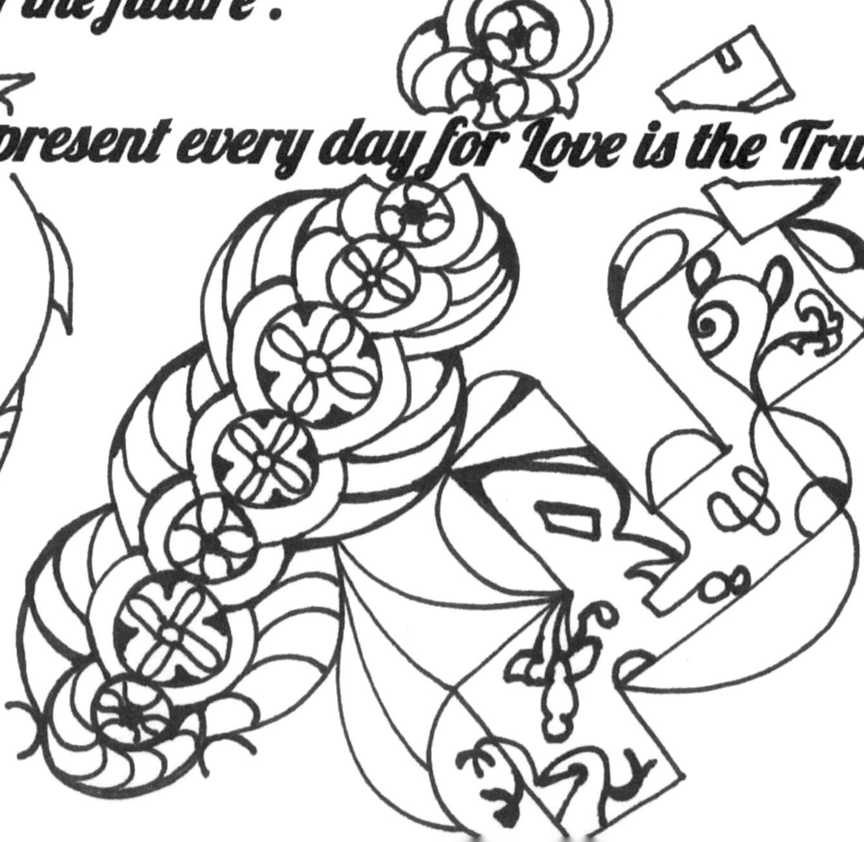

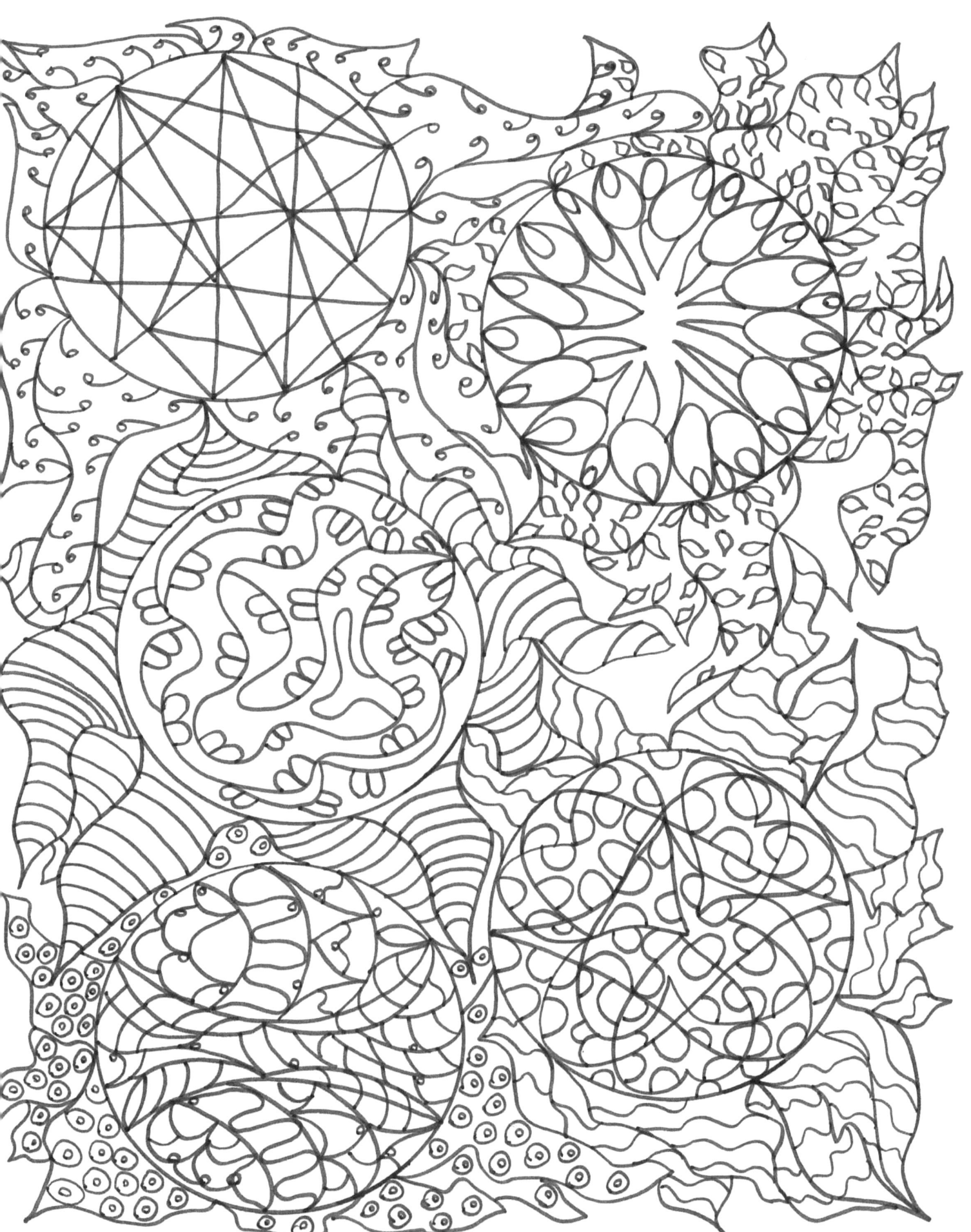

LOVE, KINDNESS and COMPASSION
Vol. 1

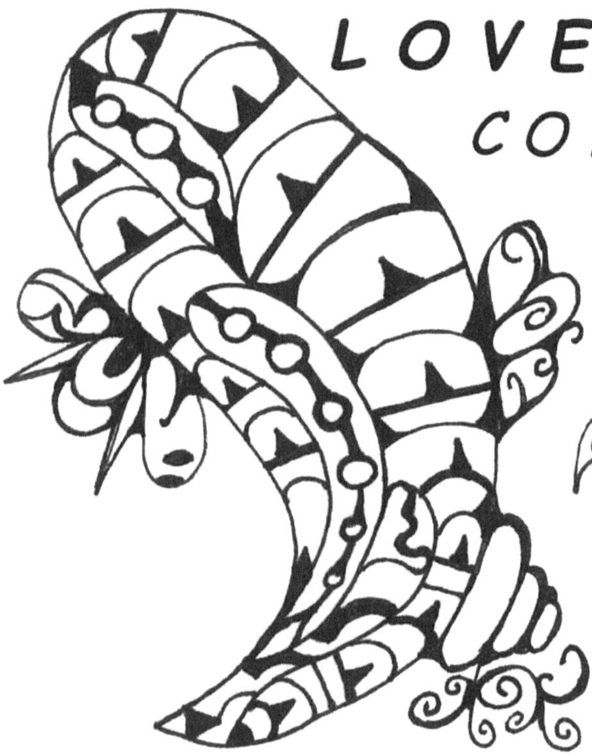

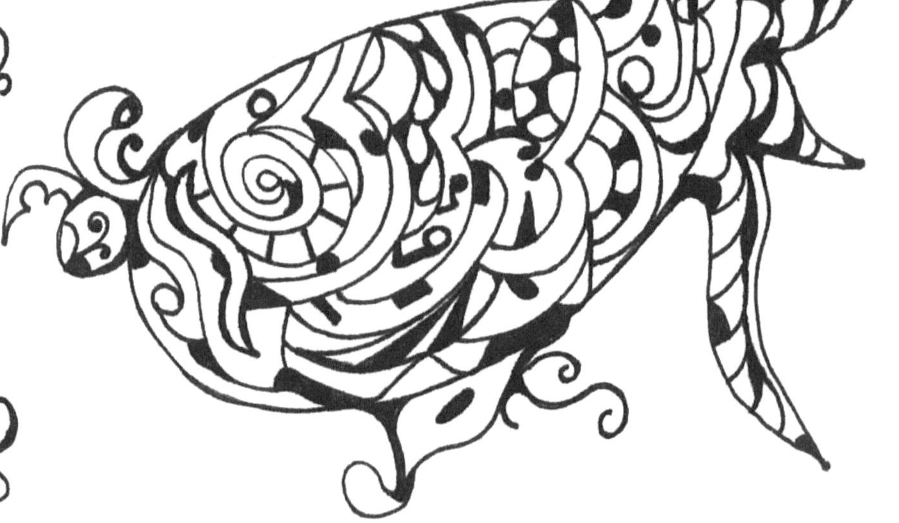

Exploratory Pages and Techniques

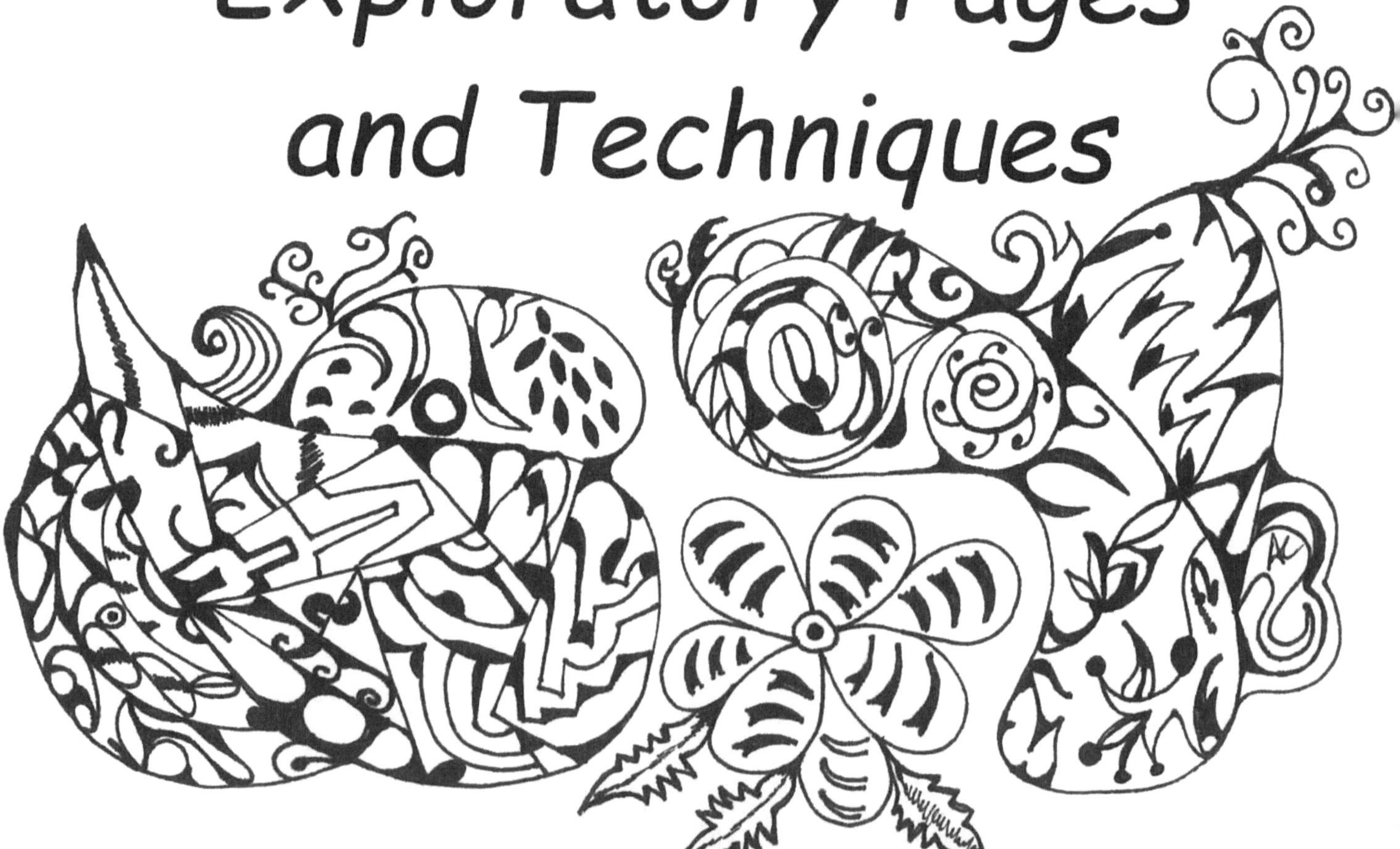

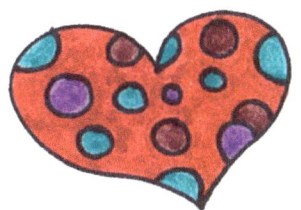  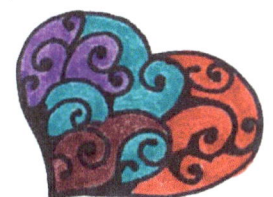

Within all of us is a divine creator!

Artwork is a self-expression from the heart. Our beliefs, feelings and desires come out when we draw. I discovered art to be one of the best forms of self-care anyone can do.

I've enclosed 5 additional partially drawn pages for you to experiment with. These pages were inspired by my years of exploration with my doodles and drawings. I took great pride and joy exploring what was inside me wanting to come out! Hence, why I've included these for your inner artist to play with!

Suggestions while drawing/doodling

First, when it comes to creating retire to a quiet place where you won't be disturbed. As much as we love our families we need time to be alone and take care of ourselves. If you can be outdoors with the sun shining, even better.

Second, maybe turn on some relaxing and calming music. However, listen to whatever floats your boat! Maybe you doodle/draw or colour to rock music!.

Third, you may want to tear the page out and make copies so you may explore creating with various pens and markers, shapes and designs. Keep the ones you love and make more!

Fourth, I have learned that the mind is calmer, relaxed and clearer if you meditate before you start. I listen to meditations specific to the Sacral (or Navel) Chakra which represents creativity.

Techniques

When it comes to technique we are all unique and our execution is neither right nor wrong. I didn't even know I had certain techniques until I put my pen to the paper. Drawing comes from within and I go with what feels good.

Pens vs. Markers.

Some of these pages were done with pen, others with markers. Some thin, others thick. I find a variation between the two works nicely. Normally after I meditate I have a vision of a shape I want to commence with and allow whatever is coming to me land on the page.

For example, if you are drawing a flower you don't have to start at the centre with a simple circle. Draw whatever comes to mind, you can even use a square. Or, at times I start with the petals and then add in the middle. Sometimes there is no middle except where all the petals join.

Leaves are fun to apply to any shape. Inside or outside a shape. If you've never drawn before it sometimes helps to study a few pictures or go outside and study plants and let your imagination do the rest.

An interesting technique and the best advice I ever got from a friend was don't worry about mistakes. Mistakes can be turned into some of the most lovely creations ever. We are human so it makes sense they do.

To give emphasis to your drawings add rainbows, flowers, hearts or whatever you like off of the main drawing. Emphasis can also be leaving no space or leaving lots of space. Sometimes less, is more. Combine shapes with different width pens and markers to give depth and to be eye-catching.

Lastly, I learned, the hard way, not to draw all the way to the edge. Some photocopiers don't catch all your creation.

I wish you many many fun filled and healing hours of creating. Namaste

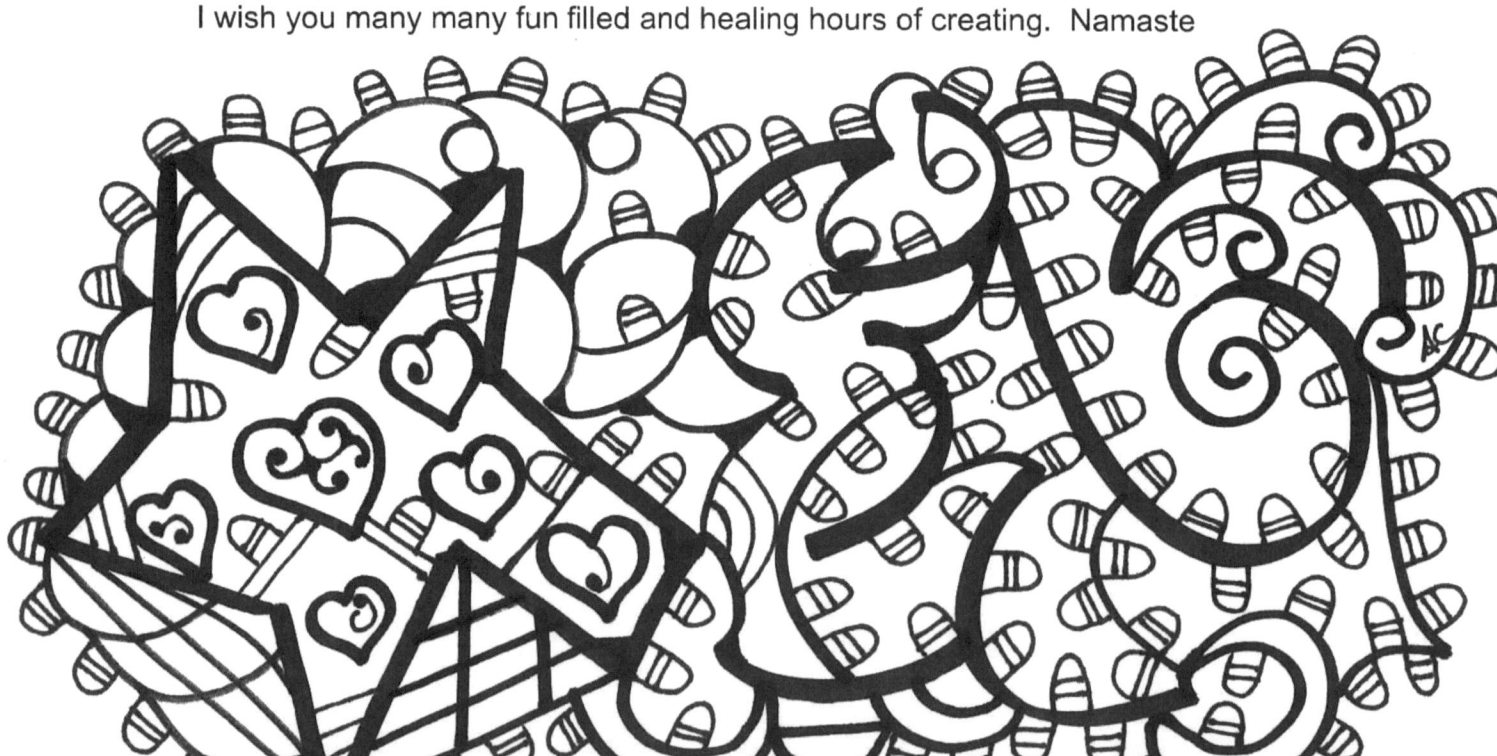

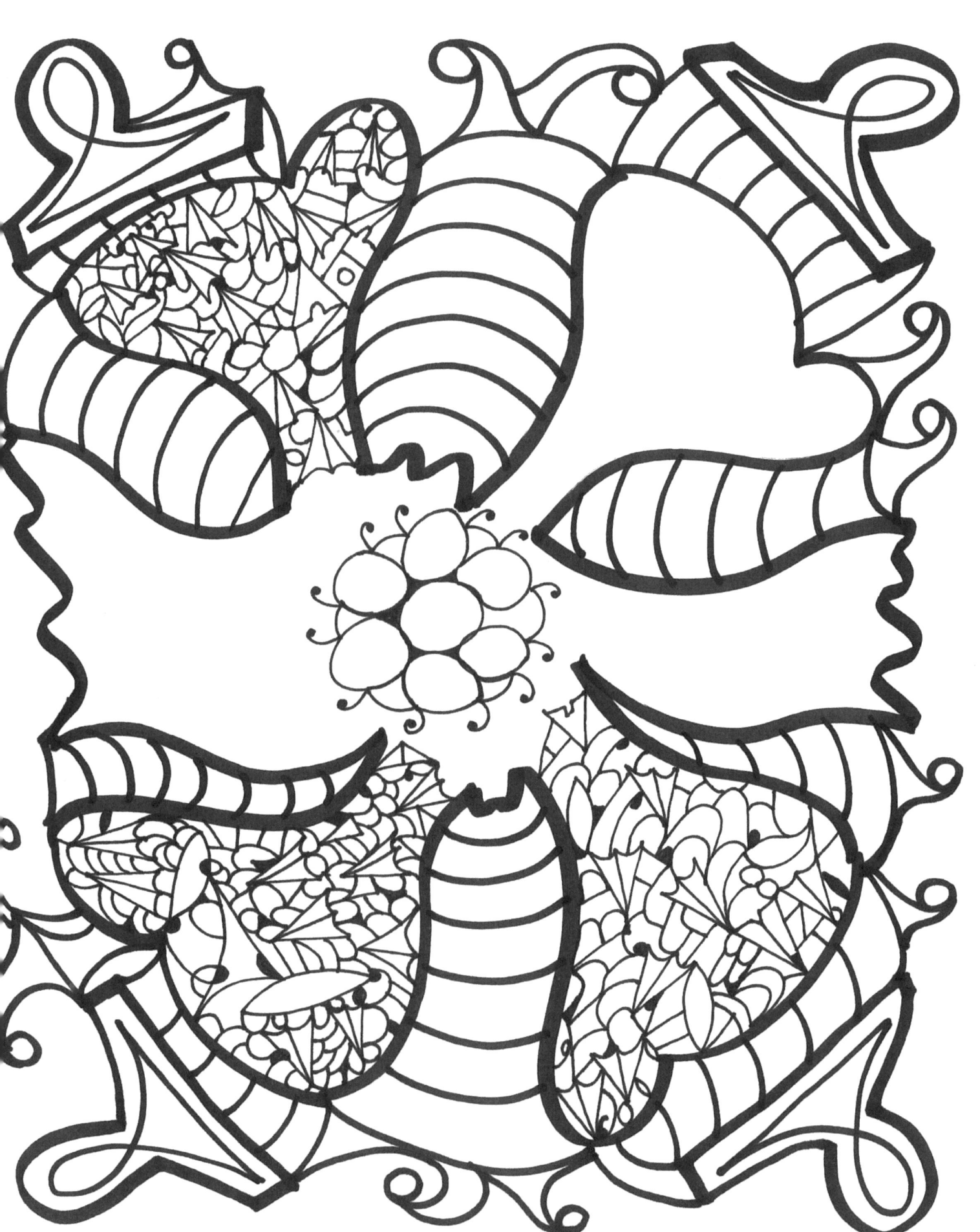

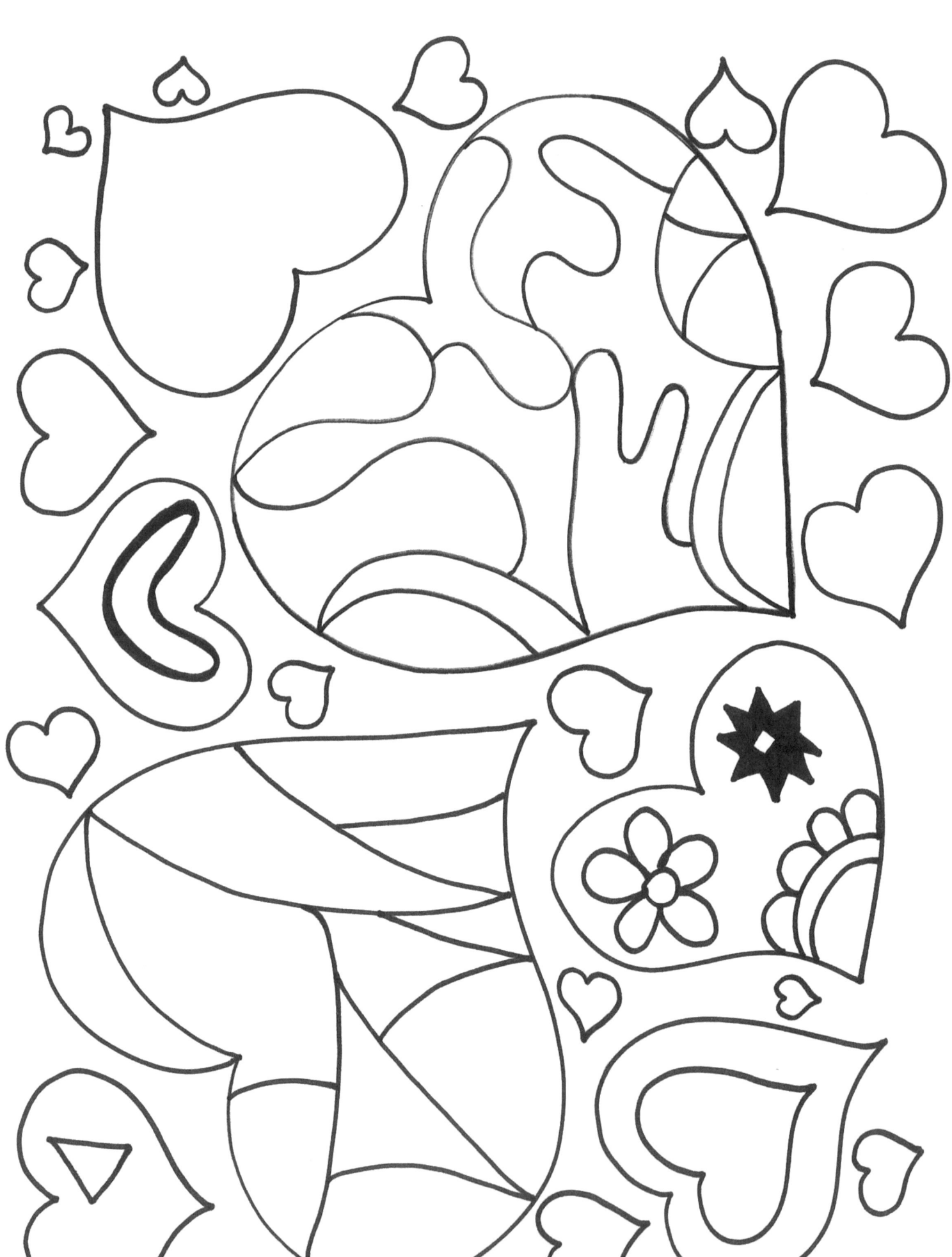

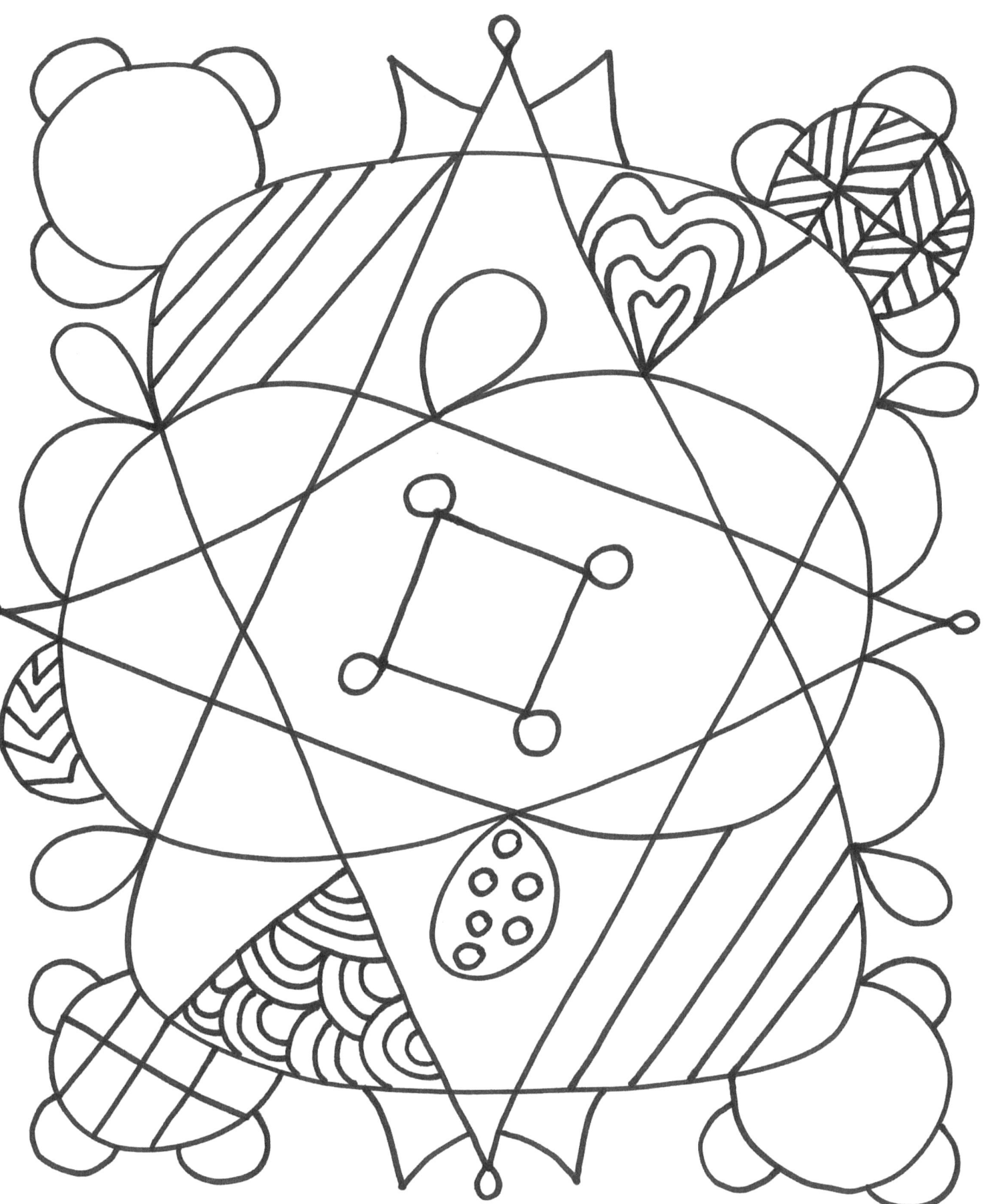

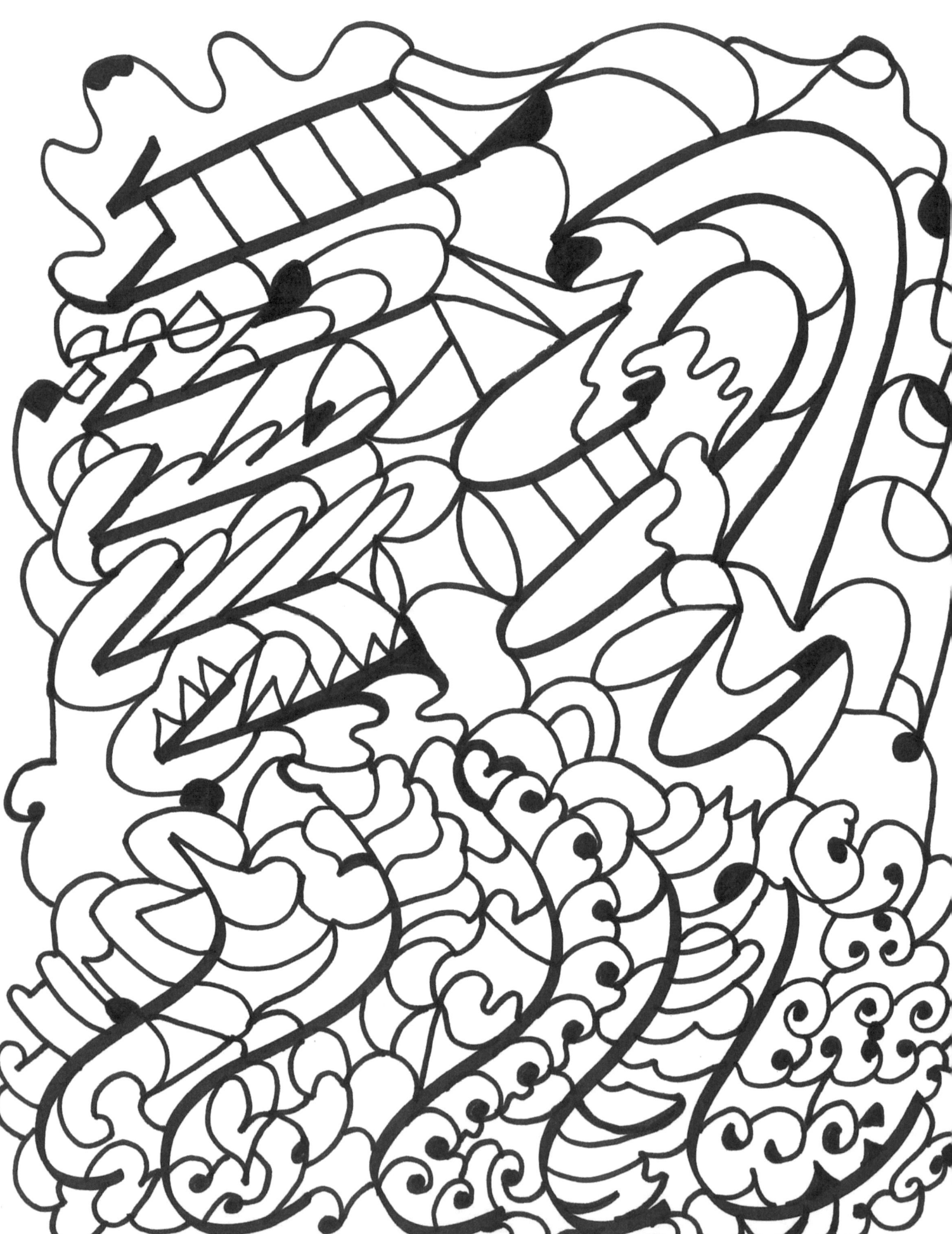

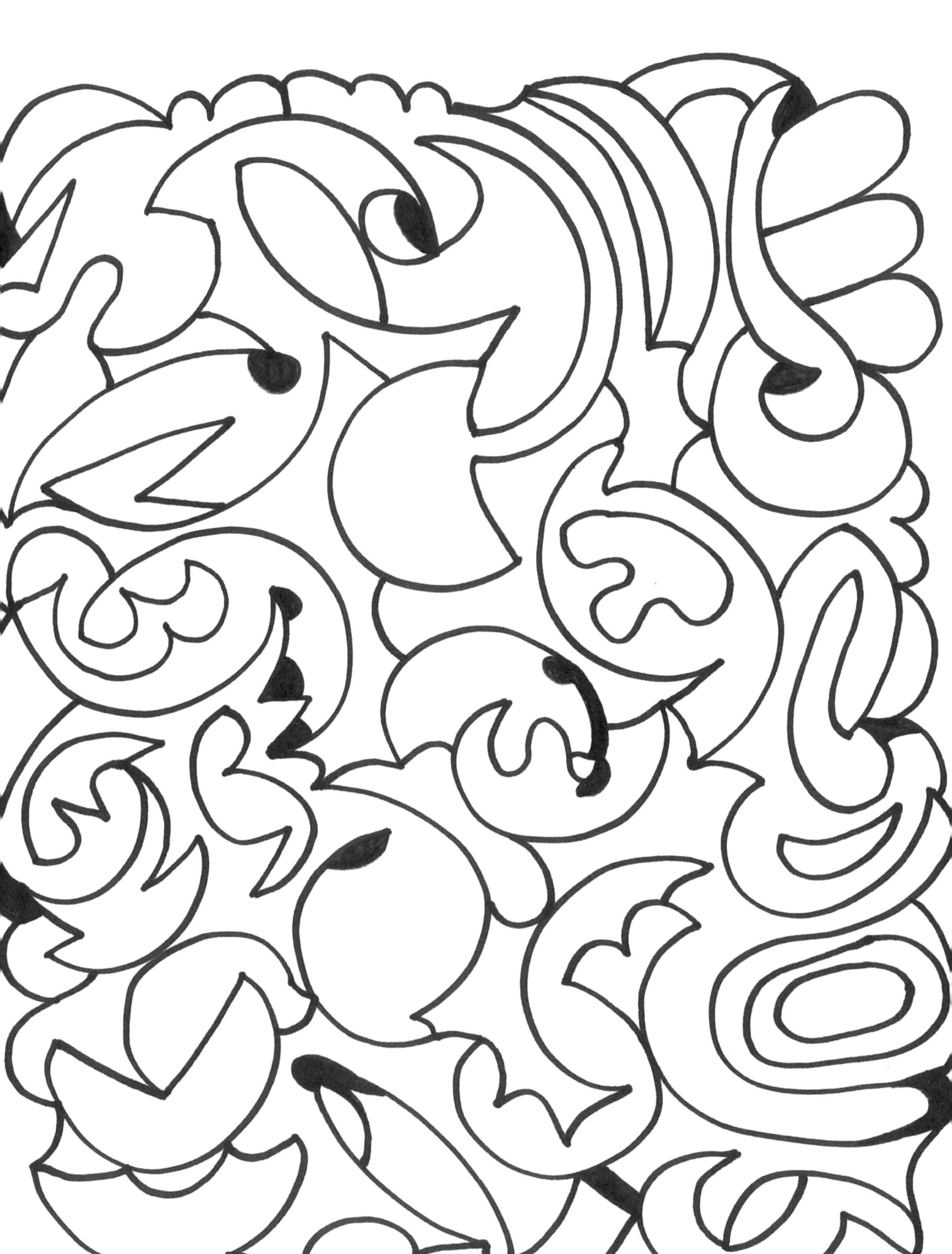

www.ingramcontent.com/pod-product-compliance
Lightning Source LLC
Chambersburg PA
CBHW040440220526
45473CB00004B/1482